AF660956

INDIA

SUSTAINABLE DEVELOPMENT AND GOOD GOVERNANCE ISSUES

A CASE FOR RADICAL REASSESSMENT

INDIA
SUSTAINABLE DEVELOPMENT AND GOOD GOVERNANCE ISSUES
A CASE FOR RADICAL REASSESSMENT

BINAYAK RAY

ATLANTIC PUBLISHERS AND DISTRIBUTORS

Published by
ATLANTIC PUBLISHERS AND DISTRIBUTORS
B-2, Vishal Enclave, New Delhi-110 027
Phones 5413460, 5429987

Sales Office
4346/4C, Ansari Road, Darya Ganj,
New Delhi-110 002
Phones 3273880, 3285873, 3280451
Fax 91-11-3285873
e-mail gupta.atlantc@axcess.net.in

Distributors in Australia, New Zealand
and the Pacific
BIBLIOTECH
(A Division of Anutech Pty. Ltd.)
The Australian National University,
ACTON ACT 2601 Australia

Copyright : The Author, 1999

ISBN 81-7156-746-0

*No part of this book may be reproduced
in any form without permission from the
publisher except for the quotation of
brief passages in criticism*

Typeset at
APD Computer Graphics, Delhi

Printed at
Mehra Offset Press, Delhi

Dedication

To the Memory of my late father,

Dhirendreswar Roy,

and my late uncles

Tripureswar Roy,

and

Himangshu Kumar Pal,

whose insistence on value based education has been a source of unerring inspiration.

I gratefully acknowledge the research assistance provided by Messrs Nur Ahmed (primarily population and employment sections) and K.K. Sanyal (primarily energy section) in preparing this book.

My appreciation is also due to The Australian National University for the opportunity given to me to work in the Department of Political and Social Change and the National Centre for Development Studies as a Visiting Fellow.

Foreword

For some time—at least since the 1960s—there has been a tendency to pay scant attention to the social and political aspects of economic growth. This has been so despite the demonstration that civil strife can hugely undermine economic growth (*vide* Sudan, Somalia, Burma [Myanmar], Sri Lanka, Cambodia or Indonesia) and that political repression and corruption can often either inhibit growth or give rise to gaps between rich and poor which create a potential for civil strife. This tendency has been only partly rectified by a growing interest in question of 'good governance' (which for the most part assumes the existence of legitimate governments capable of responding to demands for reform).

More particularly, it has been widely assumed both that the existence of democratic political system facilitates economic growth (a proposition for which the experience of post-colonial states provides little evidence, and which has been contested by Singapore's elder statesman Lee Kuan Yew) and that rising levels of economic well being promote political participation and the emergence and consolidation of democratic institutions (a provision for which also the evidence is thin).

In this context, India provides an interesting case study. A large country, riven by ethnic, religious, cultural and class cleavages, it is nonetheless one of a very few post-colonial states to have maintained an unbroken record of democracy. Yet until recently it does not appear to have been able to realise its economic potential. In the past few years, however, coinciding with a liberalisation of trade and investment, there has been evidence of a shift to higher levels of economic performance, and predictions that, in the early 21st century, the Indian economy will be among the 'big five'.

In this study Binayak Ray challenges some of the more optimistic projections of India's development. At the outset he emphasises the distinction between growth and development and income and capability. He asks: can India achieve a high economic growth rate on a sustained basis? And, if so, will it be able to achieve significant development for its entire population or will the benefits of growth be available to a limited segment of the population. Among the prerequisites for sustainable development, he argues, are a stable government which is accountable for its policies and actions and capable of organising a clean administration supported by predictable economic and social policies, an independent judiciary, and commitment to be part of the international civil society.

As areas of specific concern Ray lists population growth, the quality and stock of human resources, access to energy resources, and agrarian land reform. But beyond these more immediate concerns his study is concerned with fundamental questions of governance. For a long time India has suffered from what Ray describes as 'an unholy nexus between rent-seeking business, self-seeking politicians, and unresponsive bureaucracy'. This has resulted in widespread lack of confidence in the political process and in politicians, police and those generally in position of power and authority. Ray specifically identifies problems in the operation of the federal system, in the activities of political parties (which 'have not only failed to provide political leadership [but]...have failed to observe democratic principles in administering their parties'), in what he describes as a lack of separation between government and bureaucracy, and in the capacity of the judiciary (which apart from having a backlog of some 25 million cases in 1996, has been increasingly susceptible to political manipulation). These are linked in a broader discussion of corruption.

Ray concludes with a call for reform, identifying four principal forms: constitutional, administrative, fiscal, and public service.

This is a timely study, by an economist whose extensive public policy and administrative experience has not only sharpened his sensitivities to the critical role which social and political factors play in development, but has given him a broad range of comparative data to augment his deep-seated appreciation of the complexities of the Indian situation.

R.J. May
Senior Fellow
Department of Political and Social Change
Research School of Pacific and Asian Studies
The Australian National University

Preface

We are living in an age where changes in all walks of life are taking place at an unprecedented rate. It would not be an exaggeration to say that no country can afford to develop its economic and social policies in isolation from policies taken elsewhere.

The recent turmoil in South East Asian economies has clearly demonstrated that administrative and policy failures in one country can adversely impact on the well-being of other countries. Furthermore, the combined impact of such shortcomings in a small number of countries can even threaten global economic stability as well create regional political instabilities.

Within this context the importance of an economically and politically stable India cannot be over emphasised.

India's economic progress since independence in 1947 is impressive although somewhat patchy. Its spectacular success in the food production area—from a food deficit country to a net exporter of food products—is an example. Its democratic form of government, in spite of many weaknesses, is the envy of many countries which are struggling to preserve an open and democratic government. Notwithstanding these successes, its failures are equally many. There are disturbing signs which indicate that unless corrective measures are taken soon to overcome these deficiencies, the situation may go out of control and its achievements will be undermined and shortcomings will threaten the very foundation of the country's economic, social and political stability.

Another major area of concern is that many have failed to make a clear distinction between economic growth and development while examining India's achievements and future prospects. Assessments such as 'India will become an economic power house' in the 21st century indicate the inadequacy of such judgements. For example, Indonesia during the last decade recorded spectacular economic growth and yet within a short period it has virtually become a basket case of economic impoverishment and political instability.

This clearly shows that spectacular economic growth on its own does not necessarily mean that development is taking place. The book focuses on this issue and argues that, even if India sustains a high economic growth rate, which is doubtful, overall it may not achieve development beneficial to many of its citizens.

Besides India's high population growth rate, the biggest problem appears to be its institutional failure to maintain peoples' confidence in their capacity to uphold peoples' rights and respond to their needs and grievances. Amongst many, the failure to develop healthy constitutional conventions, to uphold supremacy of the Parliament over the executive arm of the state and the government, and to unequivocally preserve the supremacy of the judiciary are a few.

The book examines why this has happened and what options are available, short of any major political upheaval, to overcome the current situation, which many independent observers believe is reaching a crisis point.

The book, although it comments on the past economic performance and the future prospects, has as its main governance issues and how they are impacting on the economy. Constitutions (when there is written one) or constitutional conventions (as in the United Kingdom) are implemented through the administrative and judicial apparatus in all countries. The book argues that this relationship has virtually broken down, reflecting inappropriate functioning by political parties, institutions and powerful individual groups. These are adversely impacting on India's development efforts, and unless addressed urgently and decisively India, in all probability, will fall behind other countries in the development race. The book suggests that India must critically look at its constitutional, administrative and institutional apparatus to ensure that the confidence of its citizens are restored in the state and government machineries. This confidence is considered essential for sustained development in all countries, more so in India.

I have received significant encouragement, support and assistance from a large number of people in writing this book. Mr C.R. Irani, Editor-in-Chief, *The Statesman* (Calcutta and New Delhi) gave his valuable time to provide an insight into the shortcomings of the administration, institutions and how these are undermining peoples faith in the political process. Dr Ron May, Senior Fellow at the Department of Political and Social Change at the Australian National University gave many hours of his valuable time to discuss development related administrative issues which I found invaluable in identifying the critical constitutional and administrative areas requiring urgent attention. Dr M. Govinda Rao of the Australian National University also provided useful insights into how the performance of the Indian political economy can be improved. I thank all of them for their assistance.

I thank Dr R.N. Ghosh of the University of Western Australia (former A/Professor and Head of the Department of Economics) and Dr D.K. Dutta of the Department of Economics, University of Sydney for their useful comments on an earlier draft of the book. My sincere thanks are also due to Dr S.K. Mukherjee of the Australian Institute of Criminology for his useful assistance in developing ideas on how best to combat institutional corruption in the public arena. My thanks are also due to Professor A.K. Datta (Indian Institute of Public Affairs), New Delhi for his useful assistance in tracing administrative reform initiatives in India.

I also thank Central and State government officials, academics and researchers who kindly consented to be interviewed and provided valuable material for this book in 1997. As most of them agreed to be interviewed on the condition of anonymity, I have not mentioned any individual names.

My thanks are also due to the management of the *India Today* (Weekly), New Delhi who conducted the nationwide survey to asses what Indians think about the achievements in the post-independent India. The survey results provide a clear picture of what many Indians feel about the economic and political situation in India. Without this survey it would have been difficult to clearly establish the validity of my contention that sustainable development and good governance issues require a radical reassessment in India.

I most sincerely thank Ms Tracey Hansen for her painstaking editing of the draft. Her efforts have undoubtedly improved the readability of the book.

Last but not least I sincerely thank my Mother, colleagues and friends who have constantly provided encouragement to address some of the development issues in an objective way for policy considerations. I hope and trust that the book meets their expectation, if not wholly at least partially.

The Australian National University

Contents

List Of Tables

Symbols used in Tables

n.a.

Abbreviations

BBC	British Broadcasting Corporation
BCI	Bell Canada Incorporated
BJP	Bharatiya Janata Party
CBI	Central Bureau of Investigation
CII	Confederation of Indian Industry
CPM	capability poverty measurement
CPR	contraceptive prevalence rate
DAC	Development Assistance Committee
DIC	Discipline Inspection Commission (China)
DPSP	Directive Principle of State Policy
EIU	Economic Intelligence Unit
EU	European Union
FCRA	Foreign Contribution Regulation Act
FICCI	Federation of Indian Chamber of Commerce and Industry
G8	Canada, France, Germany, Italy, Japan, Soviet Russia, United Kingdom and United States.
GDP	gross domestic product
GNP	gross national product
HDI	human development index
IAS	Indian Administrative Service
ICAC	Independent Commission Against Corruption (Hong Kong)
IMF	International Monetary Fund
ISI	Indian Statistical Institute
JPC	Joint Parliamentary Committee
MCC	Merchant Chamber of Commerce
NGO	non-government organisation
OAS	Organisation of American States

ODA	Official Development Assistance
ONGC	Oil and Natural Gas Corporation (India)
PL480	United States Public Loan 480
PPP$	purchasing power parity
SAARC	South Asian Association for Regional Cooperation
TFR	total fertility rate
UN	United Nations
UNDP	United Nations Development Programme
UNICEF	United Nations International Children's Emergency Fund
WTO	World Trade Organisation

Unless otherwise mentioned, all currencies in the text are in US dollars.

Chapter One: The Parameters

I Preamble

Many economic and political commentators including the World Bank predict with guarded optimism that India will be among the big five economies in the 21st century.[1] The other four projected big economies are China, Brazil, Indonesia and Russia. It is, however, worth noting that in 1993 although ranked seventh largest among the developing economies, India's annual GDP growth was third lowest among them, ahead of the Russian Federation and Mexico only (World Bank 1995:22–9). A big economy does not necessarily mean that economic growth will lead to a higher degree of overall development and that the growth rate can be sustained.

Policy makers often fail to recognise the distinction between growth and development. While growth is an essential precondition for development, there is no guarantee that a higher growth rate automatically leads to development. The debate on the distinction between growth and development raged in the past, and is unlikely to be resolved to the satisfaction of all economists and policy makers. Growth is measurable and can be defined ordinally, whereas development cannot be defined in such a way. While the debate is unlikely to be resolved to everybody's satisfaction, there exists broad agreement that development includes consideration of factors such as how development is achieved, and incorporates qualitative aspects of human life (Gupta and Ghosh 1992:1–32). In the 1990s the United Nations Development Program (UNDP) took this issue further by developing the human development index (HDI), is a simple average of the life expectancy index, educational attainment index and adjusted real gross domestic product (GDP) per capita purchasing power parity (PPP$) index (UNDP 1997:122). The distinction between economic growth and development becomes clear from the HDI of countries which shows that higher GDP per capita does not necessarily mean high HDI ranking (Table 1). For example, in 1993 and 1994 Canada achieved highest HDI ranking although it ranked 6th and 8th respectively in real GDP per capita rank (UNDP 1996:135–7; 1997:146–8). This

---

1 World Bank, 1997. 'Global economic prospects and the developing countries', in *India among 'Big Five' Economies,* The Statesman Weekly, 13 September, Calcutta.

makes clear that in the contemporary world development commands a wider definition than that attributable to growth.

The distinction between growth and development became clear from the UNDP's development of capability poverty measurement (CPM) in 1996. The CPM is a multidimensional measure of human deprivation in three basic capabilities namely

- to be well nourished and healthy
- for healthy reproduction
- to be educated and knowledgeable (represented by female illiteracy).

It emphasises the deprivation of women as this adversely affects the development of families and society. The UNDP found that 900 million people in developing countries were income poor, but 1.6 billion people were capability poor. India's situation was one of the worst when compared with the 15 other countries investigated by the UNDP. In India 25.4 per cent of the people were income poor, but 61.5 per cent of the people were capability poor (UNDP 1996:26–7). The deprivation of women in India by any standard of measurement is extreme and this result is not entirely unexpected.

Table 1: Human development index (HDI) ranking of India, China, Indonesia and their relative position with the highest and lowest ranked countries during 1990–97

Country/ Year	HDI score	HDI ranking	HDI score	HDI ranking	HDI score	HDI ranking
	1990	1990	1996	1996	1997	1997
Japan	0.996	1st out of 130 countries	..	..	..	..
Canada	..	..	0.951	1st out of 174 countries	0.960	1st out of 175 countries
Niger	0.116	130th	0.204	174th	..	..
Sierra Leone	..	..	..	..	0.176	175th
India	0.439	93rd	0.436	135th	0.457	138th
China	0.716	64th	0.609	108th	0.629	108th
Indonesia	0.591	76th	0.641	102nd	0.668	99th

Source: UNDP 1990; 1996; 1997. *Human Development Reports*, OUP, New York.

This book addresses two basic issues. First, can India achieve a high economic growth rate on a sustained basis? Secondly, if it can, will it be able to achieve significant development for its entire population or will the benefits of growth will be available to a limited segment of the population?

To achieve sustained development, a high level of investment is required. But, investment is only one of many requirements. The other essential prerequisites are: a stable government which is accountable for its policies and actions; the government's capacity to organise a clean administration supported by a predictable economic and social policy; an independent judiciary; and a commitment to be part of the international civil society.

II Sustainable Development: Definitional Limits

The sustainable development concept is relatively a new phenomenon in development vocabulary. It received currency through the environmental movement but more importantly through the gradual realisation that firstly, there is an urgent need to integrate our environmental and developmental needs more closely; secondly, the life styles of both affluent and non-affluent nations need to be adapted within the earth's ecological means; and finally, that environmental issues cannot be considered in isolation of development issues, they are interlinked as articulated in the Brundtland Report (World Commission on Environment and Development 1987:XIII–IX, 1–23).

Following the publication of the Brundtland report, a significant number of researchers have attempted to examine this issue to develop the concept further for policy actions. However, although everybody agrees that there exists a need to integrate environment and development more closely, and that there is a need to ensure '...this generation makes sure it leaves the next generation a stock of capital no less than that available to the present generation' (Thistlewaite and Davis 1996:1–5), there remains disagreement on how much sacrifice current generation should make on equity grounds for the future generation.

The issue is further complicated by man's ingenuity and inventive capacity which may enable new technologies to replace some of earth's vital non-renewable resources such as fossil fuels. For example, it is reported that Mexico started producing passenger cars in February 1998 that run on compressed air. The car is designed to run on highly compressed air, 300 litres of which can be pumped in to a tank in three minutes at an electricity cost of less than $2. The car is also capable of cleaning polluted air, as its carbon filtering system lets the car suck in the surrounding polluted air while it is braking and 'breathe out' purified air.[2] Notwithstanding this, it is undeniable that the current state of inequitable consumption of natural resources is a mindless exploitation of our heritage that cannot be maintained unless humanity does not want to care for its future generations. This conflict between today's people and tomorrow's people needs to be addressed in a balanced way, if conflicts are to be avoided. Conflict in Australia between environmentalists and the forestry industry, which culminated in the blockage of the Australian Parliament House by the forestry industry workers in 1995, is an example. Again, compromise reached at the Kyoto environment conference in December 1997 on the allowable limits to green house gas emission targets is another example of why the sustainability issue needs to be approached cautiously.

Even at the theoretical level some people have challenged the concept's focus. The 1989 Nobel laureate in economics, Professor Solow, pointed to the paradox connected with the popularity of the sustainability concept, when he wrote

Those who are so urgent about not inflicting poverty on the future have to explain why they do not attach even higher priority to reducing poverty today? (Solow 1996).

Within this context Brundtland's comment that the focus of development should be consistent with future as well as present needs and that this process is not easy or straightforward, and '...in the final analysis, must rest on political will' (World Commission on Environment and Development 1987) is understandable. For the purpose of this book 'sustainable development' is defined as a rate of economic growth that is required to ensure a steady and long term improvement in the standard of living of a population at large (Ray and Ghosh 1997:331–51) both in absolute and comparative terms.

The task in India is enormous. Firstly, its real GDP per capita (PPP$) in 1994 was only $1,348, ranking 143rd among 175 nations, compared to China's $2,604 (1.9 times), Indonesia's $3,740 (2.8 times), Japan's

---

2 Webster, P., (1998). 'The solution to pollution: a car that runs on air', *Canberra Times*, Canberra, 25 January.

$21,581 (16 times), Canada's $21,459 (15.9 times), USA's $26,397 (19.6 times), and UK's $18,620 (13.8 times) (UNDP 1997:146–8). Secondly, its population density of 3.016 persons per hectare in 1993 is one of the highest in the world, close to that for Japan and Belgium. Only six other countries have higher densities than India—Mauritius, Rwanda, Bangladesh, South Korea, Singapore and Netherlands (World Resources 1994:284–5). Given that 73.2 per cent of India's population were living in rural areas in 1995; that 64 per cent of India's labour force were engaged in the agricultural sector in 1990 (World Bank 1997:220); and that nearly one third of India's population is living below the poverty line, addressing environmental and sustainability issues is a complex and difficult task for policy makers.

Estimates of people living below the poverty line vary widely. One estimate puts the figure at more than 200m in 1997 (Indira Gandhi Institute of Development Research 1997:4–5). The World Bank estimates that 312m (35 per cent of the population) were living in absolute poverty in 1993–94 (World Bank 1997b:i–vii). Recently a new study by researchers at the Indian Statistical Institute (ISI) found differences between the estimates made by the Government's own Central Statistical Organisation and the Institute. Both estimates were based on the same methodology. The ISI researchers sought some clarification from the Central Statistical Organisation on aspects of their calculations, but are yet to receive a response.[3] Notwithstanding these varied estimates, it is clear that a very high proportion of India's population lives in absolute poverty. Furthermore, India's progress in fighting poverty has been modest in comparison to some of her Asian neighbours.

III Good Governance—What It Means

Good governance issues gained currency in the development debate mainly through the concerns of multi-lateral agencies, donor countries and through the activities of non-government organisations (NGOs), which became concerned about the lack of transparency and accountability in governments' dealings and decision making processes, lack of human rights in some Asian, African and South American countries, and about widespread corruption in government. In

3 Aiyar, S.S.A., (1998). 'Did UF fudge poverty data to discredit Congress?', *The Economic Times*, New Delhi, 23 February. Reporting on a study by Messrs Gangopadhaya, Jain and Dubey.

addition, internal struggles against oppressive and dictatorial governments in some developing countries crystallised the importance of good governance issues and associated civil society values in maintaining peace, encouraging development and fostering human rights.

Developed countries through their membership of the Development Assistance Committee (DAC) of the Organisation for Economic Cooperation and Development (OECD) have also been pushing *good governance* issues for some time, mainly prompted by domestic pressure to ensure that aid funds provided by these countries benefit people and not the ruling elite class. In 1993, DAC in a draft policy paper stated

> ...[it is] increasingly apparent [that] there is a vital connection between open, democratic and accountable system of governance and respect for human rights, and the ability to achieve sustained economic and social development (DAC 1993: 28–30).

In a subsequent document in 1995 DAC acknowledged that it was a complex issue and identified four elements of good governance (DAC 1995). In nutshell these are:

- maintaining the rule of law: a predictable legal environment, with an objective, reliable and independent judiciary
- sound public sector management: management decisions and practices are transparent and economically sound
- controlling corruption: firmly established institutional and legal mechanism to effectively deal with corrupt practices
- avoiding excessive military expenditure: excessive military expenditure can result in conflict and repression, contribute to instability in the region and divert scarce resources from development needs.

The World Bank also lends its support to this issue, albeit indirectly as its charter does not allow it to interfere in other country's internal affairs. It pressures countries to adhere to good governance principles through its conditional program lending, which is often reinforced by IMF/Bank cross-conditionality (Singer 1993). Its view on these issues became clear when it stated that good governance was a transparent process, a bureaucracy imbued with a professional ethos; an executive arm of government accountable for its actions; a strong civil society participating in public affairs and, all behaving under the rule of law (World Bank 1994).

The World Bank's annual conference on development economics in 1991 amongst other issues considered that of good governance. The deliberations at the conference were succinctly summarised by a participating government member.

The quality and effectiveness of government enhance the state's capacity in strategic areas that are vital to the process of development. The just exercise of authority is one. A capacity for problem solving and conflict resolution is another. And the efficient performance of its functions based on the involvement of a societal coalition for development is another (Elgardo 1992:267–302).

The Development Assistance Committee and World Bank's views carry strong weight in the international political and economic arena. Many in developing countries do not fully agree with some of their specific concerns. In particular, their emphasis on Western liberal human rights issues has created resentment in some developing countries and in certain cases consternation. While disagreement between developed and developing countries on the emphasis on the human rights aspects of good governance remains, the intrinsic value of the concept cannot be ignored. However, from a conceptual point of view good governance is difficult to define—Root, while examining the successes of the East Asian economies, found that it evades definition (Root 1996:145).

Perceptions of what constitute good governance may therefore differ from country to country and person to person. A simple one line definition of good governance could be that governments should not only be effective in economic, social and political terms but they must also be owned by the citizens at large. Within this broad definitional frame there exists scope to vary policy direction, but the main focus must remain undiluted. In practical policy terms the core elements of good governance practices could be

- achieving stated economic goals
- strict adherence to laws and regulations of the country
- transparent decision making process and
- responsiveness to the needs of its citizens including acknowledging their right to elect and dismiss government i.e., free and fair elections at regular intervals to elect government.

Contrary to the difficulties of having a consensus definition of good governance, symptoms of poor governance on the other hand are easily identified although some differences on their detailed interpretations may exist. These are

- failure to make a clear separation between public and private interests; hence a tendency to divert public resources for private benefit—leads to the growth of corrupt practices in public life
- failure to establish a predictable framework for law and government behaviour, conducive to development—encourages arbitrariness in the application of rules and laws
- excessive rules, regulations, licensing requirements etc. which impede the functioning of markets—encourages rent seeking and corruption and discourages competition
- priorities inconsistent with development—resulting in misallocation of resources; excessively narrowly based or non-transparent decision making.

While acknowledging the possibility of disagreement on the universal validity of these symptoms, if the symptoms occur together with severe intensity, they create an environment hostile to development. When development fails to occur, gradual erosion of civil society values become a real possibility. In such an environment, political forces and governments tend to ignore democratic and civil society values. This in turn tends to progressively erode the authority of governments over their peoples (World Bank 1992:33–4).

Chapter Two: The Economy and Some Areas of Concern

I A Bird's Eye View Of The Past

India's strident effort to achieve economic growth and development began with the establishment of the Indian Planning Commission in 1951 which, with the Prime Minister as its Chairperson, guided development activities through a series of five-year plans. The First five-year plan was launched in 1951. The plan was mainly one of public expenditure for development purposes and ground preparing type for increased productivity and reduction of inequalities (Ghosh 1997:63–136). The Second five-year plan focused on industrialisation, emphasising public sector investment and heavy and strategic industries. The focus in subsequent plans reflected the government's economic and social priorities at the time of their formulation. Five-year plans were suspended during 1966–69. Instead, annual plans were operative which encompassed the basic framework of the Fourth five-year plan. This suspension was caused by a number of factors amongst which the Indo-Pak conflict of 1965, consecutive droughts and the devaluation of the currency were significant. The Eighth plan concluded in March 1997.

Implementation of the Ninth plan has been delayed. This is due to the dissolution of the Lower House of the Indian Parliament in December 1997. Planning Commission sources indicated that as the care-taker government did not enjoy the authority to clear the draft plan incorporating recommendations for serious policy implications, the formal implementation would be delayed until the new government adopts the plan for implementation.[4] Until the draft plan is approved, annual plans will be formulated and implemented.

From an ideological point of view, the policy focus of successive five year plans did not vary significantly until the Eighth plan when the Government initiated a number of policy shifts with the objective of removing constraints on industrial growth and providing a more liberal economic environment for the development of industries. Prior to this, economic policy was dominated by restrictive practices such as control through licenses, permits, high tariffs and exchange control. In spite of

---

4 Bhatia, S.L., 1997. 'Polls send 9th Plan to 2-yr holiday', *Economic Times*, New Delhi, 10 December.

these restrictive practices, India achieved limited economic success during this period, particularly in the agricultural sector. Its success in the agricultural sector has been impressive, from a food deficit country in the 1960s, it is now a net exporter of food products. This, however, has failed to significantly reduce the number of people living below the poverty line.

The success of the agricultural sector was mainly due to factors such as the introduction of high yielding variety seeds and the easy availability of fertiliser not to any radical initiatives such as land reform. The initial breakthrough was achieved in Punjab and Haryana but by the end of the 1970s, began to spread to other parts of India (Ghosh 1977:94–113). In addition, the delay in the supply of food under the PL480 program in the late 1960s by the Johnson Presidency, and a committed techo-bureucratic agricultural leadership also contributed to achieving this success (Lewis 1995:79–131).

The biggest drawback of the Indian economy was its insular nature; its failure to open-up the economy to compete globally. Prior to the 1991 economic crisis the economy virtually remained isolated from the global economy with the government retaining unlimited power to dispense favour to business houses and industries (Ray and Ghosh 1997:331–51). This made the economy unresponsive to consumer needs, made it a captive of a system it created and protected, which has been patronised by an unholy nexus between rent seeking business, self seeking politicians and unresponsive bureaucracy. The foreign exchange crisis forced a radical shift in economic policy in 1990–91 to create a more competitive economic environment by freeing government control on many aspects of economic operatives. To a large extent this has broken the shackles of a rigid and inefficient economy, and has forced a psychological shift to look at the economic parameters from a totally different perspective. India watchers like Lewis, however, argue with some justification that pro-liberalisation of the Indian economy actually started in the late 1960s. His focus was however limited to the food production sector. While there is unlikely to be full agreement on his claim, there cannot be any disagreement with his other point that successful reforms must be indigenously rooted (Lewis 1995:159–60).

India's limited economic success however does not compare favourably with the successes achieved by other big countries in the neighbourhood such as China and Indonesia (until recently). India, China and Indonesia began their journey to achieve rapid economic and social development virtually at the same time: India in 1947, China in

1949 and Indonesia in 1945. These are all complex societies and were subjugated to colonial rule. An examination of key economic indicators shows that until the Asian financial crisis in late 1997 both China and Indonesia achieved much faster growth rates than India. Their political leadership, initially at least, had a similar eco-political objective, although the political systems followed by these three countries are different. There could be a legitimate argument that China and Indonesia's higher economic growth rates were made possible by their somewhat contrived political system which denied their citizens certain basic human rights. While there may be some truth in this argument, it nevertheless cannot be the sole reason.

In terms of growth of per capita income, level of unemployment and people living in poverty, India's achievement during past decades has been below that of China and Indonesia. In 1973 India's per capita income was the highest in South Asia and higher than Indonesia (data for China are not available for 1973). By 1993, India's per capita income was lowest among these three countries: China's per capita income was more than one and a half times India's, and Indonesia's was nearly two and a half times higher (recent turmoil in the Indonesian economy has not been taken into account). India, a dominant economy in South Asia, also recorded a lower per capita income growth rate compared to South Asia as a whole. India's growth rate was even lower than the growth rate recorded by low income economies (Table 2).

Table 2: Growth of per capita GNP during 1973–93 in India, Indonesia, China, South Asia and low income economies (Aus$)

Country / Year	1973	1980	1993
India	130	250	300
Indonesia	120	490	740
China	..	280	490
South Asia	130	250	310
Low income economies	..	310	380

Source: World Bank 1995. *World Tables*, John Hopkins Press, Baltimore.

This poor record can be attributed to a very poor income growth for rural labour. The 1993–94 Rural Labour Inquiry Report found that the average daily earnings of farm labour households increased in real terms by only 10 *paise* during last 30 years, a meagre 2.5 cents in 10 years (based on an exchange rate of one US$ to 40 Indian Rupees).[5] About 73 per cent (678 million) of India's estimated population of 929 million was living in rural areas in 1994.

The rate of unemployment is another indicator of the health of an economy. India had a very large number of registered unemployed in 1992. As there is no universal social security system, it is neither obligatory nor necessary for Indians to register if they are unemployed. India's registered unemployment figure, if anything, is therefore likely to be under recorded. Professor John Lewis who has spent significant time in India and observed the development of the Indian economy from a very privileged position and from close quarters found that

> There is an enormous if unmeasured amount of unemployment and underemployment in the system; it unquestionably has been rising from Plan to Plan (Lewis 1995:188).

Indonesia's number of unemployed was small (this situation changed dramatically following the 1997 economic turmoil) and China's unemployment figure covered only urban unemployed, but the figure is comparatively small (Table 3). However, China's unemployment situation has started deteriorating rapidly with its decision to move away from a command economy to a market economy. With the reform of the state-owned enterprises it is estimated that some 12 million urban state workers have already been made redundant. The Chinese Trade Union Federation estimates that another 10 to 12 million jobs will be lost by 2000 as a consequence of these reform processes.[6]

---

5 *Hindusthan Times,* (1997). 'Slight rise in real income for farm labour in 30 years', (Sixth Rural Labour Inquiry Report of 1993–94), New Delhi, 31 December.

6 Poole, T. (1998). 'Unemployment reaching crisis levels in the new-age nation', The *Canberra Times*, Canberra 6 March.

Table 3: Number of employed and registered unemployed people in India, China and Indonesia (million)

India	1992	27.06 *	36.76
China	1994	614.70 **	4.76 ***
Indonesia	1994	79.9	1.3

*Notes: *Refers to applicants currently registered at employment exchanges. ** Refers to social labour force that generates income including total staff and workers, employees in urban private enterprises, urban individual labourers, rural labourers and other social labourers. *** Refers to urban unemployment only.*

Source: Asian Development Bank 1996. Key Indicators of Developing Asian and Pacific Countries, OUP, Manila.

The most distressing and disturbing economic indicator is the large number of people living below the poverty line. In absolute and percentage terms, the number of people living below the poverty line in India is highest in the world. During 1989–94 more than one half of India's population was living with an income of one dollar or less a day, compared to 29 per cent in China and 15 per cent in Indonesia (Table 4). In 1993–94, out of 312 million people living below the poverty line, 240 million were rural poor and the remaining 70 million were urban poor. A matter of significant concern is that while the government has introduced a number of anti-poverty programs, many of the poorest were not using these programs while many of the non-poor benefited from them (World Bank 1997b:vi–vii). This could be due to many things: poor program design and/or implementation; lack of focus; poor administration or just simple corruption.

Table 4: Percentage of population living in poverty in India, China and Indonesia

Country	Living with one dollar a day or less in 1989–94	National poverty line
India	53	..
China	29	11
Indonesia	15	8

Source: UNDP 1997. *Human Development Report,* OUP, New York.

Even though in money terms a significant proportion of the Indian population was living below the poverty line, a more disturbing point is that the state has failed to provide even the essential basic services to them without which they are not able to come out of the poverty trap and social deprivation. This became clear from the human poverty index as measured by the UNDP. On this basis India occupies 47th position out of 78 countries whose poverty index was measured by the

UNDP (UNDP 1997:126–7). In other words, there were only 31 countries worse than India, compared to 60 countries below China and 55 countries worse than Indonesia. Out of a total of five indicators of human poverty, only in one category (people without access to safe water) was India's record better than either China or Indonesia. In the remaining four, India's position was well behind these two countries (Table 5).

Table 5: Human poverty index in 1997 for India, China, Indonesia and their world ranking (%)

Country	Rank	People not expected to survive to age 40 (1990)	People without access to health service (1990–95)	People without access to safe water (1990–96)	Adult illiteracy rate (1995)	Children not reaching grade five (1990–95)
India	47th	19.4	15	19	48	38
China	18th	9.1	12	33	18.5	12
Indonesia	23rd	14.8	7	38	16.2	8

Note: A total of 78 countries were measured.

Source: UNDP 1997. *Human Development Report*, OUP, New York.

This failure to provide the basic necessities of life to the economically poor has a number of social consequences. The most important of these is that the deprived community cannot feel empowered to exercise their basic human and political rights, particularly when they are economically and socially dominated by privileged classes such as the landed gentry, traders and money lenders. Furthermore, without this empowerment they will not be able to assert their rightful place in society, which is a basic prerequisite for their self-esteem, an essential factor for growth and development. India's adult literacy rate of about 49 per cent is not only significantly higher than China and Indonesia, it was even higher than the sub-Saharan rate in 1994. In 1970 India's adult literacy rate was 34 per cent compared with sub-Saharan Africa's rate of 27 per cent; in 1994 the rates were 51 per cent and 56 per cent respectively (UNDP 1997:166–7). A recent Indian study found that empowering women through education would go a long way in alleviating poverty (Dubey and Gangopadhaya 1998).

Amongst many things contributing to them remaining capability poor is the skewed income distribution and poor literacy rates. In 1993, 25 per cent of India's population were considered 'income poor' but at the same time 62 per cent were found to be 'capability poor' (Table 6).

Table 6: Percentage of population classified as income and capability* poor in India, China and Indonesia in 1993 (%).

Country	Income poor	Capability poor
India	25.4	61.5
China	10.9	17.5
Indonesia	16.7	42.3

*Note: *Capability poverty is measured by taking into account (i) capability to be well nourished and healthy, represented by the proportion of children under five who are under weight; (ii) capability for healthy reproduction, proxied by the proportion of births unattended by trained health personnel; and (iii) capability to be educated and knowledgeable, represented by female illiteracy. In capability poverty index measurement India ranked 89th, China ranked 24th and Indonesia ranked 62nd out of 101 countries measured.*

Source: UNDP 1996. *Human Development Report*, OUP, New York.

India recorded an annual GDP growth rate (at constant market prices) of 5.4 per cent between 1980–81 and 1985–86; 5.9 per cent between 1985–86 and 1990–91. It dramatically declined to 0.8 per cent in 1991–92, and following the economic reforms introduced it increased to 6.4 per cent during 1992–93 and 1995–96 (World Bank 1997c: economic development data). In 1997–98 the Reserve Bank estimated that the growth rate could be about 6 per cent. However, this estimate was made before the full impact of the down turn in the Asian economies is felt. As mentioned earlier the impact of this downturn on the Indian economy is likely to be significant, particularly in the export sector. In general, exports have been declining for some time. In 1995–96, export grew by 24.5 per cent but declined to only 6.4 per cent between April and December in 1996–97 and further declined to 3.3 per cent during the same period in 1997–98. While monthly balance of trade figures are not a reliable trend indicators, nevertheless a declining export with increasing import remains a matter of concern. In December 1997 exports further declined by 5.1 per cent and imports increased by 11.9 per cent. The trend therefore is not very encouraging at this stage.[7]

GDP growth rate on its own does not always provide a clear indication of countries economic health. It needs to be looked at along with net value of all overseas financial transactions, and the population growth rate to establish whether the national as well as individual economic situation is improving. India's high population growth rate eats up even this meagre growth, and hence the overall standard of living is not

7 *Hindusthan Times* (1998), New Delhi, 8 January and 5 February.

increasing in any significant way. Annual gross per capita growth rate (GNP) was only 1.5 per cent during 1965–80 and 3.0 per cent during 1980–93 (UNDP 1997:203).

II A Bird's Eye View Of Future Prospects

How the Indian economy will perform during next two to three decades is virtually impossible to predict, particularly as it gradually opens to international competition and becomes a part of the global economy. No econometric model realistically can incorporate all variables impacting on the direction and shape of the economy. The hazards of such predictions are borne by recent events in Asia. Economic commentators including multilateral development and funding agencies until recently were very confident about the prospects of the Asian tiger economies. However, within a six month period this euphoria has not only vanished, but the concern has shifted to ensure that this melt-down does not drag the world economy in recession.

The hazards of forecasting are also clear from the International Monetary Fund's (IMF) revised December 1997 *World Economic Outlook*. There it admitted that originally it had misjudged the extent of the Asian economic turmoil. It did not see any reason to be pessimistic about the world economic prospects, but reduced the estimate for overall world output for 1998 by about one percentage point (from 4.3 to 3.5). The OECD has also warned that this meltdown will adversely impact on the growth level of other economies (Peake 1997). Only 11 months earlier the OECD predicted that all 29 member countries would enjoy economic growth in 1997, for the first time since 1985, and developing countries were also expected to achieve a similar growth trend.

The anecdotal evidence indicates that the Asian crisis was to a large extent created by a number of factors such as corruption at high levels (not by clerks alone at the desk level), widespread cronyism, inappropriate policy setting, relaxed lending policies of financial institutions, the proliferation of non-income producing projects, failure of regulatory agencies to properly administer their supervisory powers, and the absence of a transparent policy development procedure. The Transparency International survey of businesses' perception of corrupt practices in various countries found that in 1995 two of these 'tiger economies,' South Korea and Indonesia scored 4.29 and 1.94 respectively out of a possible score of 10 for an extremely clean country (Root 1996:ix–xvii). While Indonesia was last amongst 41 surveyed countries, India's position was seventh lowest with a score of 2.78. Indonesia's and South Korea's dramatic economic decline to a large extent is attributed to wide spread corruption and a non-transparent policy environment. India's corruption level is close to Indonesia's, and the issue is yet to be effectively and firmly addressed. Indonesia's corruption has not yet been openly and effectively addressed as it was in South Korea where even former presidents were successfully prosecuted.

Domestic savings, investment in new technology, modernisation of the existing manufacturing sector and improvements in productivity are keys elements for achieving a sustained economic growth rate. India's current domestic savings rate of a little over 20 per cent falls short to meet the investment requirements during next few decades. However, a quick estimate by the Central Statistical Organisation (CSO) in February 1998 puts the figure to be 26 per cent of GDP.[8] The figure appears to be wild guess, but if it is true and the savings are managed properly, the economy will benefit from it. While India's current private domestic savings rate is comparatively high, it is yet to be firmly established whether with the opening up of the economy, this savings rate can be sustained.

Some of the middle-class demand for high-value consumption goods which remained unmet during last few decades suddenly may find openings via easy availability of goods and services. Anecdotal evidence indicates that overseas recreational travel, education and medical treatment by the affluent middle-class may negatively influence the achievement of a higher private domestic savings rate. The position still remains unclear, and the situation must be continuously monitored to adjust fiscal and other policies appropriately in the event domestic savings rate shows a declining trend. Singapore is perhaps only one of the very few countries which managed to fund its investment requirements through a high domestic savings rate of 45 per cent of its GDP. However, Singapore's management of its national affairs including administrative efficiency is well recognised. India remains well behind in terms of administrative efficiency, policy transparency and a corruption-free administration.

8 The *Economic Times* (1998), New Delhi, 7 February.

Another important social factor which governments would find practically impossible to influence is Indian's penchant for gold. This social custom not only holds up key capital which could be used for economically productive purposes, but also diverts foreign exchange to pay for imported gold. No accurate estimate of the quantity of gold privately held is possible, but it is believed to be in the order of about 12,000 tonnes, outside the Central Bank and gold-related commercial operations. In earlier days one finance minister tried to restrict private consumption of gold without success. It is a social issue and can only be tackled by a judicious mix of fiscal policy and social engineering. Currently the government has liberalised gold imports to curb the activities of smugglers, but this policy needs to be executed in conjunction with other policies discouraging gold hoarding if it is not to '...lock up even more of India's private investable surplus in an unproductive choice' (Chakrabarti 1997).

A very significant portion of the required investment capital will have to come from overseas during next few decades. However, in spite of the increasing interests shown by foreign investors, India has not yet been able to create a momentum of foreign investors preferring India as a place to invest. Until this psychological environment is created foreign capital in comparative terms will remain shy of India. In spite of the government's reform of economic policies, their administration remains a major management concern. Multi-national companies such Bell Canada (BCI) which started a joint venture with a well known Indian company (Tatas) to provide basic telephone services and won a license in 1995 has now decided to withdraw from India on the ground that doing business in India means struggle at every step.[9] The impact of this decision on other potential investors should not be underestimated. In the early 1990s many investors made the same complaint and withdrew from India. It appears that the Government of India is unable to embrace the administrative changes which must accompany any policy change to attract overseas investment.

In 1995 net private capital flow to India was $3,592 million, a little over four fold rise on 1980 flow of $868 million. Comparatively China recorded a net inflow of $44, 339 million in 1995, more than 12 times India's net inflow. In 1980 net inflow to China was only $1,732

9 Jain, A., 1998. Reporting from Toronto in the *Economic Times*, quoting a press interview by the Vice President of the Company, New Delhi, 2 March.

million (World Bank 1997:218). Perception is an important element in attracting foreign investment. In spite of political differences with capital exporting countries, China has been able to print in their minds that it is a good place for investment. In 1997 according to press reports it recorded a capital inflow of $62 billion, a rise of more than 10 per cent over the previous year. The amount includes $43 billion of direct investment, $12 billion in loans and $7 billion in stocks and bonds.[10]

Even if it is assumed that the necessary capital is available, the absence of adequate and appropriate physical facilities and in many cases the poor quality of existing facilities may not make it possible for the economy to absorb the investment. The Indian Government appointed an expert group on Commercialisation of Infrastructure Projects in 1994 to examine the infrastructure issue. The Committee in its report in 1996 estimated that in each of the eight years beginning 1998–99 and until 2005–06 gross domestic investment required in the infrastructure sector would be 27.3 per cent of GDP rising to 31.5 per cent in the last year (Government of India 1996:Vol. II:48). This is only at the macro level. Additional investments required at the micro level are also considerable, particularly in the housing and urban services sectors.

An important source of investment funds, many believe, is overseas aid. However, growth theorists agree that for foreign aid to be effective, it must be of the right type and targeted efficiently, and its success to a large extent depends on the capacity of the recipient government to use the aid efficiently (Walker 1996:16).

In India's case overseas aid is unlikely to play a major role because even at the best of times, aggregate official development assistance (ODA) to developing countries did not exceed 2 per cent of their aggregate GDP. In 1994, India's receipt of ODA was only 0.8 per cent of its gross national product (GNP) declining to 0.6 in 1995 (UNDP 1996:172–86; 1997). Given that the amount of ODA has steadily declined over the years and is still declining, and that in global terms there are many more 'basket cases' than India whose demand for assistance will receive priorities on humanitarian and political grounds, India's prospects for increased ODA are not bright. Furthermore, empirical research found that all political regimes allocate foreign aid in

---

10 The *Economic Times*, 1998. 'Inflow of foreign capital into China at record high', New Delhi, 5 January.

favour of a high-income political élite rather than the poor (Boone 1995). Given India's experience with the PL 480 program during the Johnson Presidency (Lewis 1995:92–114), it would be appropriate to assume that unconditional foreign aid is a myth,[11] and hence non-availability of large amounts of ODA may be a blessing in the long-run.

Concerning whether a sustainable growth rate can be maintained, anecdotal evidence indicates that short to medium term future may not be as bright as many optimists would like to believe. For example, the Reserve Bank has already downgraded its forecast of GDP growth to 6 per cent in 1997–98 compared to its earlier forecast of 7 per cent.[12] However, the latest estimate by the Central Statistical Organisation puts the figure at 5 per cent, a decline of 2.5 per cent over the previous year.[13] These estimates were made before the full impact of the turmoil in the 'tiger economies' on the Indian economy is felt. According to its estimates, negative growth is expected in the agriculture, forestry and fishing sector, with growth in all other sectors except mining and quarrying declining; community, social and personal services sector.

A matter of serious concern is the possibility of exports shrinking in the short to medium term as a result of a decline in world trade. In 1995 world trade grew by 20 per cent, but declined to only 3.3 per cent in 1996. The Economic Intelligence Unit (EIU) now estimates that world trade will increase by only 2.9 per cent in 1998, compared to 4 per cent in 1997.[14] One of many reasons for this dramatic decline was high unemployment in many developed economies such as the European Union. Even in Japan where imports were up by 22 per cent in 1995, trade shrank to a mere 4 per cent in 1996.

This distressed export scenario is further complicated by the discriminating trading by regional economic groupings where member countries are given preferential trading facilities contributing to the dramatic decline in exports at a time of economic uncertainty in many countries. Panandiker nicely summed up the situation 'We export more only when the world imports more' (Panandiker 1997). India is not yet

---

11 For an interesting discussion on use of foreign aid as a political tool, see Jonathan Power's (1997) article under the same heading in *The Statesman*, Calcutta, 22 August.

12 *The Economic Times*, 1997. 'RBI scales down GDP growth forecast at 6 per cent', New Delhi, 26 December.

13 *The Economic Times*, 1998. New Delhi, 24 February.

14 *The Economic Times*, 1998. New Delhi, 11 February.

a part of any such economic block. Even if trading is liberalised within the South Asian countries (SAARC), significant benefits cannot be expected because first, none of the SAARC economies are growing fast; second, the economies of SAARC countries are not complementary to the extent that trade can increase quickly; and third, trading between them would not bring in the hard currencies which all developing countries need to finance their imports from outside SAARC.

Anecdotal evidence further indicates that many manufacturers are not able to fulfil their expectations. For example, the giant white goods manufacturer in India, Whirlpool, has sustained huge losses for two consecutive years, and has now applied for deferment of its royalty payment to its parent company in the USA.[15] In a growing economy where the middle-class does not have many of the modern-day domestic white-goods as in western society, the company would not have suffered such an ignominious situation if the economy had been performing according to its expectations. Many other manufacturing companies are also in an uncomfortable situation, but none as bad as Whirlpool.

Within this context the November 1997 survey by the Federation of Indian Chambers of Commerce and Industry (FICCI) clearly shows that the perception of business was depressing. The earlier May 1997 survey showed that 75 per cent of the surveyed business houses believed that the business slowdown would be temporary, and there would be a turnaround within six to nine months. The November survey showed that 44 per cent of the respondents believed that it would last more than a year, and only three per cent of the companies were optimistic that the gloom would lift in the next six months.[16]

The Confederation of Indian Industry (CII) has also recently commented that the economic and industrial climate in India is very difficult in 1998, although it declined to confirm that it was as bad as 1991 when India faced a foreign exchange crisis and was forced to introduce reform

---

15 *The Economic Times*, 1998. 'Loss-stricken Whirlpool to defer royalty payment', 19 January, New Delhi.

16 FCCI survey (1997), reported in The Economic Times, 24 December, New Delhi. This survey was conducted before the extent of the East Asian economic crisis was known and its implications were realised or fully understood.

measures.[17] Another study by the Merchant Chamber of Commerce (MCC) concludes that India is expected to reel under industrial slowdown for more than a year. It concludes that at best industrial growth would be around 7 per cent, but it also looks ambitious at this stage.[18] The latest Central Statistical Organisation estimate for the average growth rate during the first nine months of 1997–98 is pegged at close to 4.7 per cent, well below the 8.6 per cent achieved during the previous financial year.[19]

There are a number of issues to be looked at. First, India's trading pattern during the 1981–96 period confirms Indonesia, Malaysia, Philippines, Thailand, Korea, Singapore and Hong Kong as India's main trading competitors (World Bank 1997c:45). Except for Singapore and Hong Kong all these countries have recorded massive devaluation of their currencies which will make their exports very cheap compared to other countries including India. Compared to the depreciation of Indonesian, Thai, South Korean and Malaysian currencies, depreciation of the Indian currency was relatively small. Therefore, in all probability India is likely to face much tougher competition. It will be very difficult to compete with exports from these countries which will enjoy a price advantage due to the massive devaluation of their currencies. Conversely, India's top eight markets will also find it cheaper to buy from India's competitors. Except Singapore, all these countries traded commodities similar to India's. In a meeting between the South East Asian diplomats in India and Indian business and industry associations, envoys predicted that the Asian crisis will adversely hit Indian exports.[20]

Second, and more importantly, the massive devaluation of the currencies of these countries and the failure of many of their enterprises to meet their loan repayment commitments will make it very attractive for foreign investors to buy these enterprises at bargain prices. This could take place in a number of ways, for example increased equity participation or funding newly restructured industries which would be less risky, particularly in the context of a reformed financial and administrative environment. Foreign investors are unlikely to let this

---

17 Sayed, J., 1998, reported in the *Economic Times* quoting the Director General, CII, New Delhi, 26 February.
18 *The Economic Times,* 1998. New Delhi, 10 February.
19 *The Economic Times,* 1998. New Delhi, 18 February.
20 The *Economic Times,* 1998. New Delhi, 24 January.

massive opportunity go. India will have to compete with them to attract foreign investment for at least the short to medium term.

Third, all these countries have agreed to pursue stringent economic austerity, reform their administrative structure and improve their regulatory mechanism as conditions for the IMF guaranteed bail-out package. Although many of these measures will create severe social tension and crisis, governments will have no option but to follow them with iron-fist determination. Most of these conditions involve more interference in national economic affairs on the grounds of structural reform (Wright 1998). Although these conditions are a form of invasion of sovereignty, in the global economic context investment hungry countries hardly have any real choice where capital is extremely footloose, competition for market share is severe and new technology is essential for staying competitive in the market place. Inevitably, imposed reform proposals often demand removal of subsidies, clean administration, labour discipline and a predictable policy frame. These create tension within individual societies and require strong political leadership.

The critical issue for India, therefore, is can it handle the social turmoil which massive restructuring of the Indian economy will inevitably lead to. Restructuring will lead to massive downsizing of the labour force which will bring significant pain to many middle-class workers, particularly in the financial and other organised sectors of the economy. Although of the estimated labour force of 398 million in 1995 (World Bank 1997d:43), only 27.5 million were employed in the organised sector (World Bank 1997c:7), the power of the organised sector to disrupt the normal working of the economy is significant. For example, average number of work days lost per year per employee in the manufacturing sector during 1982–92 period was significantly higher than five of India's seven trade competitors. India lost 5.736 work days per year per employee compared to Indonesia's 0.010; Thailand's 0.039; Malaysia's 0.004; Korea's 0.216; Philippines 0.646 and nil for Singapore (Indira Gandhi Institute of Development Research 1997:160).

Demand for higher wages without significant improvement in productivity will require a strong administration to handle such situations. The political and social turmoil in Thailand, South Korea and Indonesia in particular clearly exemplifies the need for a strong government to ensure that the conditions imposed by lending agencies are implemented. However, political uncertainty created by loose coalition governments and inept political leadership will make it extremely difficult, if not impossible, to pursue such policies. The Indian government's capitulation in granting huge salary increases to its own staff without obtaining any guarantee of higher productivity or radical reform in its administrative structure is an example. It is rumoured that former Prime Minister Gujral privately expressed his helplessness to take on the powerful government employees union by refusing to grant huge increases in salaries in 1997, following the Fifth Pay Commission Report.

The huge salary increase is to be paid for by pruning development expenditure and by imposing additional taxes and duties.[21] The flow-on effect of this increase to state and local government employees is enormous. Initially it was estimated that if the central government agreed with the Fifth Pay Commission recommendations it would cost it Rs 300,000 million extra annually to pay bureaucrats at the central, state and local government levels (including teachers and health workers). As most of the states and local governments already spend more than 50 per cent of their revenue to pay salaries (some, including the Cabinet Secretary of the Government of India, estimate it to be as high as 95 per cent), hardly any funds will be left for providing services to their citizens (Mukarji 1997). The news filtering from state governments already indicates that the initial estimate of additional expenditure for salaries was significantly underestimated. A recently concluded agreement between the state government employees and the Government in one state put the additional requirement to Rs 650,000 million during the ninth plan period.[22] This estimate does not include the additional amount required to pay teachers and local government employees. This is to be seen within the background that many believe that a large proportion of employees in various government departments hardly do any productive work implying that a significant reduction (one estimate is as high as 75 per cent) in numbers would not adversely affect efficiency (Naik 1997).

Besides government employees' unions, the capacity of politically powerful middle-class labour and professions in such a political environment cannot be underestimated in India. Although other

21 The *Statesman Weekly,* 1997. 'Editorial mid year blues', Calcutta, 27 September.

22 The *Hindusthan Times,* 1997. 'Pact with staff to cost Govt. Rs 6,500 crore', New Delhi, 26 November.

economically powerful groups (e.g. small and medium-sized land holders and farmers) are increasingly asserting their political strength, the middle-class and their allies are articulate, and dominates political leadership, it does not matter which party rules. The bureaucracy and the labour leadership which is totally dominated by the middle and upper income group will use these opportunities to further their own and sectional interests.

The demand by the All India Federation of University and College Teachers' Organisation and their significant show of strength in front of the University Grants Commission office in New Delhi in March 1997 is a case in point. Nobody can dispute their grievances on many issues, but what is disappointing is that the Association's outright rejection of '...the increase in allocation of money for the basic and school education at the cost of higher education and research' (Sen 1997). Also, the Association was silent on the perceived failures on the part of its many members to meet the implied standards required of them, both in the teaching and research fields. It would have done enormous justice to itself if it had explicitly acknowledged that without improving the quality of teaching and teachers at the primary and secondary levels, standards at the university level can not improve, nor it can assure that the best brains are getting into the higher education stream. After all, the country still has the ignominious distinction of having an adult illiteracy rate of about 49 per cent, a rate higher than for sub-Saharan Africa.

Third, but more importantly in the global economic context, the health of the financial sector determines the health of the economic sector. The Indian financial sector is not only a basket case for reform, but it is riddled with corruption and inefficiency. Performance of the public sector banks in 1995–96, show that they lost Rs 11.6 billion, and return on assets was -0.3 per cent. One of these banks lost Rs 13.4 billion, alleged to have been caused by corruption at the managing director level. Out of about 30 nationalised banks, only the largest one made a profit of Rs 8.3 billion, and that too a meagre return of 0.6 per cent on its assets (World Bank 1997c:49).

The East Asian financial crisis has already prompted international financial institutions (such as the World Bank and International Monetary Fund) and G8 countries to take a much more hands-on approach in determining economic and fiscal policy directions in developing countries. They wield enormous power in determining the direction of the international financial institutions, market perceptions and the international economy. The World Bank and the IMF acknowledged that they should have been more careful and diligent in monitoring not only the economic health, but also allied institutional arrangements and the issue of corruption. The Bank President publicly apologised at a meeting in February 1998 in Jakarta for the Bank's failure to detect corruption and institutional failures.[23] Even before the recent crisis, the IMF's Managing Director vowed to fight corruption, stating that fund officials would see it as their duty to press for anti-corruption reforms in countries seeking to borrow, even if this could not be an explicit requirement for receiving IMF support (Transparency International 1997).

The economic power of this group is significant. Even Japan, which is one of the world's most powerful economies cannot ignore the collective wishes of this group. It has started giving attention to its corruption riddled financial sector following a recent spurt of failures which in many instances were created by business and political corruption. The bankruptcy of Yamaichi Securities (fourth biggest stock-broker), downgrading of Yasuda Trust (a leading Japanese Bank) to junk bond status and the failure of regional banks such as Tokuyo City Bank are examples. The serious nature of the Japanese crisis is evident as Japan's finance minister (Mr Mitsutsuka) resigned his office in January 1998 after accepting moral responsibility for his ministry's failures. At the same time a senior treasury official committed suicide, unable to face the shame of subsequent investigation.

G8 countries have already considered some stringent regulatory measures. The reported measures include (Brummer and Elliot 1998)

- tightening data requirements for member countries so there is clearer, up-to-date information on capital market positions
- an improved communication mechanism for the IMF which will allow it to voice concerns and force changes in policy in a more public way
- updating the IMF's mandate to include its role in resolving problems in the capital markets, banking ranks and sorting out balance of payments imbalances.

Within this context it would virtually become obligatory to ensure that the Indian financial system including banking, insurance and non-banking financial institutions undergo radical reform. This is

---

23 *Financial Review,* 1998. Sydney, 5 February.

emphasised because until now whatever reforms were initiated, they have been insignificant and patchy (Bhattacharya 1997) compared to those executed by developed countries. These will set the benchmark for Indian financial institutions, in terms of their operational efficiency, policy effectiveness and probity.

Corruption in India has already attracted the World Bank's attention. The Bank President in his address at an IMF meeting in Washington in April 1997 urged Indians themselves to confront their leadership on this issue.[24] Given the level of corruption both at the individual and institutional levels, it would be reasonable to expect that a significant amount of clean-up work will be required before large amounts of foreign investment could be attracted. Multi-national investors would take note of the World Bank and IMF assessments in future before taking their decision to invest in India. Undoubtedly, Indian financial institutions, regulatory authorities and policing agencies will be put under stringent scrutiny not only by the multilateral agencies but also by financial markets.

Whether living standards in India will improve during the period up to 2025 in comparison to selected developing and developed countries (China, Japan, Canada, United Kingdom and USA), depends upon whether a substantial higher economic growth rate can be achieved in relation to its population growth rate. Assuming alternative annual growth rates ranging between 4.5 per cent and 8.5 per cent for China and selected developed countries (Japan, United Kingdom, USA and Canada), and comparing their per capita gross domestic product (GDP) with India under alternative population growth rate scenarios gives a reasonable indication of where India will be placed in relation to these countries in 2025 (Table 7).

24 The *Statesman Weekly*, 1997. 'Indians urged to confront leadership', Calcutta, 3 May.

Table 7: India's estimated per capita income during 2000–2025 compared with China and selected developed countries* under alternative economic and population growth scenarios

Rate	4.50%		5.50%		6.50%		7.50%		8.50%	
	China	Rest	China	Rest	China	Rest	China	Rest	China	Rest
Year	**Scenario 1 India's GDP growing at a rate of 8.5% pa**									
	1A High population growth scenario									
2000	D	I	D	I	D	I	I	I	I	I
2010	E	I	D	I	I	I	I	I	I	I
2020	E	I	E	I	I	I	I	I	I	I
2025	E	I	E	I	E	I	I	I	I	I
	1B Medium population growth scenario									
2000	D	I	D	I	D	I	I	I	I	I
2010	E	I	D	I	I	I	I	I	I	I
2020	E	I	E	I	D	I	I	I	I	I
2025	E	I	E	I	E	I	I	I	I	I
	1C Low population growth scenario									
2000	D	I	D	E	D	I	I	I	I	I
2010	E	I	D	E	I	I	I	I	I	I
2020	E	I	E	E	D	I	I	I	I	I
2025	E	I	E	E	E	I	I	I	I	I
	Scenario 2 India's GDP growing at a rate of 7.5%									
	2A High population growth scenario									
2000	D	I	D	I	I	I	I	I	I	I
2010	D	I	D	I	I	I	I	I	I	I
2020	E	I	D	I	I	I	I	I	I	I
2025	E	I	E	I	I	I	I	I	I	I
	2B Medium population growth scenario									
2000	D	I	D	I	I	I	I	I	I	I
2010	D	I	D	I	I	I	I	I	I	I
2020	E	I	D	I	I	I	I	I	I	I
2025	E	I	E	I	I	I	I	I	I	I
	2C Low population growth scenario									
2000	D	I	D	I	I	I	I	I	I	I
2010	D	I	D	I	I	I	I	I	I	I
2020	E	I	D	I	I	I	I	I	I	I
2025	E	I	E	I	I	I	I	I	I	I
	Scenario 3 India's GDP growing at a rate of 6.5%									
	3A High population growth scenario									
2000	D	I	I	I	I	I	I	I	I	I
2010	D	I	I	I	I	I	I	I	I	I
2020	D	I	I	I	I	I	I	I	I	I
2025	E	I	I	I	I	I	I	I	I	I
	3B Medium population growth scenario									
2000	D	I	I	I	I	I	I	I	I	I
2010	D	I	I	I	I	I	I	I	I	I
2020	D	I	I	I	I	I	I	I	I	I
2025	E	I	I	I	I	I	I	I	I	I
	3C Low population growth scenario									
2000	D	I	I	I	I	I	I	I	I	I
2010	D	I	I	I	I	I	I	I	I	I
2020	D	I	I	I	I	I	I	I	I	I
2025	E	I	I	I	I	I	I	I	I	I

Note: * *United Kingdom, United States, Canada and Japan.*

I indicates per capita income gap between India and other countries increasing.

D indicates per capita income gap between India and other countries decreasing.

E indicates India's per capita income will exceed other countries' per capita income.

No separate examination of India's economic growth rate below 6.5% has been made as it consistently shows widening income gap between India and other countries. Individual comparison between India and developed countries (Rest) has not been shown separately as the trend outcome is same for all countries under alternative population and economic growth scenarios.

In this table separate estimates are made of India's per capita GDP along with the per capita GDP in China, Japan, United Kingdom, USA and Canada (in the table the last four named countries are shown together [Rest]). The alternative population growth scenarios (high, medium and low) used in this table are taken from the United Nations' projections based on alternative fertility growth assumptions for different countries (UN 1995b:144).

This table clearly shows that the gap between per capita income for India and developed countries, even with a continuous high economic growth rate of 8.5 per cent, will continue to increase. The gap will decrease if their economies fail to record any growth. This is an unlikely scenario because if developed countries do not grow it would be neigh impossible for India to achieve a high economic growth rate either. A former Member of the Indian Parliament (Roy 1997) in a recent article hypothetically raised the question when can India expect to reduce the per capita income gap with developed countries? In response, it could be categorically stated that the scenario is extremely bleak. The two main variables are economic growth rate and population growth rate. An all out effort is required to boost economic growth rate on the one hand and dramatically reduce population growth rate on the other, to make it even a remote possibility.

More realistically it would be appropriate to compare India's situation with China's. The income gap will reduce in 2010 should the Chinese economy grow at a rate of 4.5 per cent, in 2020 at 5.5 per cent and in 2025 at 6.5 per cent compared to India's 8.5 per cent. It is possible for India to surpass the Chinese per capita GDP should China be unable to maintain her relativity with India's growth rate. On the contrary, if China continues to grow either at 7.5 or 8.5 per cent, then the gap between these two countries will continue to increase all the time. The result will be same under all three alternative population growth rate scenarios.

III Some Specific Areas Of Concern

A number of important factors will significantly influence the level of economic development in India in the next two to three decades. The four most important are: population growth rate, the quality and stock of its human resources, access to energy resources and agrarian land reform. These are considered critical because policy failure to achieve the desired outcome in any of these sectors will adversely impact on

India's economic growth rate. In this section, the first three issues are examined in some detail. The land reform issue is not discussed because it is totally a political issue in India—as is clear since the Government of India announced in 1949 that it had achieved agrarian land reform, only to acknowledge later that it was a difficult task (Lewis 1995:75–76). Three states which are acknowledged to have achieved land reform are Kerala, West Bengal and Karnataka. Both Kerala and West Bengal achieved this during left wing government rule—the governments were politically committed. Karnataka historically has been a progressive even when it was a princely state. It is the odd state out; others were not able to achieve land reform. No amount of policy manipulation can achieve land reform objectives, unless political will and commitment is there. The importance of land reform in feeding the growing population is commented upon in the following section.

IIIA Population

In 1994 India's population was estimated to be 913.5 million. In 1960 it was 442.3 million. The 1950 population figures did not truly reflect the situation as the effect of partition was not fully reflected in the country's population number then. Between 1960 and 1994 India's population increased by 471.2 million; in other words, the population more than doubled in 34 years. The UN estimates that on the basis of the current growth rate the Indian population will double by 2036, compared to China's which will double by 2069 (UNDP 1997:195). It estimates that, under three alternative growth assumptions, India's population will be somewhere between 1,266.3 million (low growth scenario) and 1,501.5 million (high growth scenario) in 2025. Given current trends in birth and death rates it is unlikely that low growth targets can be achieved. Similarly, high growth estimates assume a pessimistic future, although it is not totally unrealistic.

India's family planning programs have achieved only limited success. India has failed to achieve its targets for reducing fertility rates. The National Health Policy in 1983 set a target to achieve total fertility rate (TFR) of 2.1 by the year 2000. The latest estimate by the Registrar General indicates that the country would not achieve this rate before 2026. Similarly, the contraceptive prevalence rate (CPR) is also lowest among many of the developing Asian countries. For example India's CPR of 43 stands badly against Thailand (74), Indonesia (55), Turkey (63), China (83), and South Korea (79) (Sahay 1997).

Even though the UN's projection is based on certain assumptions, the pitfalls and hazards in making such projections should be borne in mind while using these data. A slight difference in assumption in certain age cohorts or in age-sex ratio can make a significant difference in the final figures. Some of the critical areas are mortality and fertility, cohort size uncertainty and migration policy uncertainty (Lutz, Goldstein and Prinz 1996:14–44). Furthermore, the census figures on which projections are based often suffer from inaccurate enumeration. For example, the Registrar General's office has confirmed that undercounting of an average of 30 per thousand had occurred in the 1991 census, which meant underlisting three per cent of the population in 1991 of 839 million (excluding Jammu and Kashmir where no census was taken).[25]

In India's case the situation becomes further complicated because of significant differences in fertility and mortality rates between states. For example, in Kerala and Tamilnadu fertility rates were 2.0 and 2.5 respectively in 1993. In Rajasthan, Uttar Pradesh and Bihar total fertility rate varied between 3.6 and 4.8 (Cleland 1966:47–72). Significant outmigration takes place from these states to other states for economic reasons, particularly in the unskilled and semi-skilled categories. This migration will influence birth rates in the affected states and ultimately the size of the total population.

In making these projections the UN assumed separate fertility variants for each country. The medium variant is thought to be more realistic than the other two.

The pressure of such huge population increases on the land and environment will be enormous. From 1901 to 1951, the population density increased from 77 persons per square kilometre to 117 persons. Comparatively density increased from 216 persons to 267 between 1981 and 1991. In other words, there was a greater rise in density in just one decade compared to first half of this century. Six states already have reached a density of 400 persons and above per square kilometre (World Resource Institute 1994:83–106).

The increased food production required to feed these extra people will require intensive cultivation, as there will be little scope for bringing new land under cultivation. This has to be considered along with the

25 Deputy Registrar General of India, 1997. Press Statement, *The Statesman Weekly*, Calcutta, 18 October.

availability of water for irrigation and related purposes. Water sharing between the states has already become a contentious political issue. India already withdraws nearly 21 per cent of its renewable water resources (Rosengrant 1997:2). Given the direct correlation between increased income level and water consumption, competing demands on available water resources will create another layer of policy complexity. Furthermore, water is a very emotive issue, unscrupulous political leadership can use water related issues easily to create political instability and discontent.

In the absence of any scope for increased agricultural production by expanding acreage, politically sensitive issues such as land reform will also have to be dealt with. In the Indian political context, this will be an extremely difficult and complex task as the beneficiaries of a feudal land-ownership system will not peacefully surrender their privileged position. Land reform measures have been successfully introduced only in Kerala, West Bengal and Karnataka. Tenancy reform and implementation of land ceilings have remained largely unsuccessful in other states. Large states which have a poor record in human development and poverty reduction (Bihar, Uttar Pradesh, Madhya Pradesh and Rajasthan) are characterised by unequal ownership of land, absentee ownership and insecure tenancies (World Bank 1997b:12). When the situation on the ground indicates such appalling conditions in 1998, it does not invoke confidence in the government's and bureaucracies' capacity to resolve this issue successfully.

The age-structure of the projected population also will have significant policy implications as the labour force will increase significantly (Table 8).

Table 8: Estimated population to 2025 by age group under alternative growth assumptions (%)

	1995	2000	2010	2020	2025
Age group		High growth scenario			
0–4	12.79	12.14	10.74	9.24	9.25
5–14	22.61	21.87	20.35	18.44	17.23
15–59	57.43	58.49	60.54	61.99	61.99
60+	7.17	7.50	8.37	10.33	11.53
Total population (million)	938.4	1030.5	1221.7	1406.1	1501.5
Age group		Medium growth scenario			
0–4	12.54	11.66	9.81	7.77	7.76
5–14	22.67	21.79	19.60	16.96	15.25
15–59	57.60	58.98	61.98	64.33	64.56
60+	7.19	7.56	8.60	10.94	12.44
Total population (million)	935.7	1022.0	1189.1	1327.1	1392.1
Age group		Low growth scenario			
0–4	12.29	11.18	8.84	6.18	6.16
5–14	22.74	21.72	18.82	15.32	13.00
15–59	57.76	59.48	63.50	66.88	67.38
60 +	7.21	7.63	8.84	11.62	13.46
Total population (million)	933.0	1,013.4	1,156.6	1,249.7	1,266.3

Source: United Nations 1994. *World Population Projection,* OUP, New York.

Table 9: Estimated labour force to 2025 by sex under alternative population growth assumptions ('000)

Alternative population growth rates/year	Total labour force (15 to 59 age group)	Female labour force (15 to 59 age group)
High population growth rate		
2000	372,002	89,586
2010	456,452	109,926
2020	537,044	130,012
2025	551,240	117,423
Medium population growth rate		
2000	372,002	89,586
2010	454,860	109,540
2020	526,024	127,330
2025	553,193	134,309
Low population growth rate		
2000	372,002	89,586
2010	453,252	109,150
2020	514,994	124,645
2025	533,529	129,513

Note: Participation rates are assumed to be 30 per cent and 16 per cent for males and females respectively in the 15–19 age group, and 80 per cent and 31 per cent in the 15–59 age group.

Sources: (i) United Nations 1994. The Sex and Age Distribution of the World Population: the 1994 revision:439–41.(ii) World Bank 1996. World Development Report 1995:145.

In this forecast female participation rate has been assumed to remain at 31 per cent. This is a big unknown at this stage. The female participation rate in India was 30 per cent in 1970, declining to 25 per cent in 1992. Reasons for such significant decline are not yet fully established (World Bank 1994b:210–11). Economic needs, changes in the perception of the female role in society, and a global tendency towards equal opportunity are some of the reasons which are likely to induce women to participate in the work force at a higher rate. If this happens, number of people seeking jobs could be higher than the figures in the Table 9 indicate.

The working age population (between 15 and 59 years) will vary between 62 per cent and 67 per cent of the total population compared to about 58 per cent in 1995. India is already experiencing significant unemployment, which many consider the root cause of social disturbances, ethnic and sub-regional conflicts. Besides militant insurgency, increasing demands by regional political parties not to allow people from other states to seek work or study at the expense of the local people is alarming. This eventually may threaten the very survival of India in its present form. One could argue that this is a time bomb waiting to explode in the form of social unrest, adversely affecting economic growth and social cohesion. In fact, signs that this is happening are already there. The Kashmir Government which is fighting an insurgency movement publicly acknowledged last year that unemployment was one of the main reasons secessionists gained foothold in the state, through the frustration and anger among youths.[26]

The situation in other parts of the country is also causing concern. For example, recently the chairman of a central staff selection committee in Mumbai (Bombay), the financial and commercial centre of India, was forced to state in writing that he intended to cooperate with the demand to reserve 80 per cent of clerical positions and 100 per cent of menial positions for the local people. The demonstration was alleged to have been blessed by the supremo of the ruling regional political party in the state and the organisation responsible for this incident was headed by a minister, close relative of the Chief Minister of the state. The Secretary of the organisation is alleged to have argued 'It is nice to talk about national integration. But when it comes to hunger, one has to feed the child in the house first and not the neighbour's child.'[27] The message expresses a popular sentiment which is difficult to disagree with in trying circumstances. A similar movement in Mumbai in the 1960s took an ugly communal turn. It is not beyond contemplation that similar demands could spring in other parts of the country as the unemployment situation worsens. The state of Karnataka has already restricted students from other states in its higher educational institutions.[28]

The percentage of population in the age group of 60 and above will increase to between 12 per cent and 13.5 per cent compared to about 7

---

26 *Economic Times*, 1997. New Delhi, 28 November.

27 *Hindusthan Times*, 1997. New Delhi, 11 October.

28 *The Statesman Weekly*, 1997. '"Non-Karnataka" students shut out', Calcutta, 10 May.

per cent in 1995. There are three significant resource and policy implications of this huge increase.

- Currently, only a very small number of the Indian work force has access to some form of superannuation scheme, and almost 100 per cent of pension recipients are either directly employed in the public sector or one supported by public sector contributions. In the absence of any universal social security safety net there will be increasing community pressure on governments to address this issue which will be hard to ignore.
- Per capita health spending in India is currently minuscule compared to developed countries. Also, central government expenditure on health has not kept pace with population growth—in fact it has fallen in the recent years. From 1992 to 1995 central government expenditure on health declined to 1.8 per cent compared to 2 per cent in 1980 (UNDP 1997:186–7). Per capita health spending in 1986–87 ranged from Rs 15 in Bihar and Rs 44.7 in Maharastra. In this context the extra call on funds for the health sector will be significant. When the existing rural health centres and public hospitals in urban centre are suffering from a lack of resources in terms of supplies and staff, it is questionable whether the government will be able to meet this increasing pressure for health sector services. Given this resource constraint, there needs to be a significant rethinking on how to address this problem with limited resources. Experts in the field believe that current focus on expensive hi-tech medicine as practiced in the west will never be able to cope with the situation (Anita 1997). The policy focus has to change dramatically, however this is beyond the scope of this chapter.
- In the absence of universal social security arrangements for the economically poor, large families in developing countries are considered an insurance for the old age. Unless this situation changes the vast majority of the population will have no choice but to depend on family members for their old age support. A large family in that context works as an insurance. This has significant implications for the family planning program, which, given the current situation needs to be the policy priority for the government.

There is no question that unless population growth is given top priority in the development policy, other policies will not be able to achieve their objectives, as any gains will be overtaken by the rapidly increasing population. It is undoubtedly a complex policy issue as it requires focus on a number of fronts simultaneously with evangelical leadership commitments if the ultimate objective of achieving lower population growth is to be achieved. Education, empowerment of women, maternal health and child mortality via better nutrition and primary health care, and above all economic security are key issues.

Adult illiteracy remains very high amongst women. The Constitution has been amended (83rd amendment) making primary education a fundamental right. But the amendment leaves the responsibility for enforcing it to the states. Fourteen states and territories have passed legislation making primary education compulsory. Passing legislation is one thing, getting people motivated and involved in achieving these objectives is another. In India this remains a serious problem. Even the National Literary Mission which was mandated to make 100 million people in the age group of 15–35 literate by 1997, achieved only 56.1 million by 1996 (Nair 1997).

The status of women in India still remains low. This is reflected in all statistical variables where neither their participation rate nor their achievement rate is high. In rural areas even young girls remain engaged in activities such as collecting fuel, fodder and water for households at the expense of attending schools (World Resources 1994:86).

About 40 per cent of the Indian households are still affected by malnutrition. Between 1975 and 1989 the percentage of households with adequate nutrition remained the same although food production increased many times (*ibid*:85). Within households women suffer more than the male members of the family; this is a social issue as much an economic issue. Male members are seen as future income earners, and hence their preferential treatment within the household. The situation has yet to improve in any discernible way. UNICEF highlighted that India and Bangladesh share the dubious distinction of having the highest child malnutrition levels in the world in the 1997 report *The State of the World's Children*. The report went on to highlight that 'Evidence indicates that the low birth-weight of infants of the sub-continent is a legacy of malnourishment in the womb, and of the fact that the mothers themselves were persistently malnourished during their own infancy, childhood, adolescence and pregnancy.'[29] The malnutrition issue is not a simple one. Economists now agree that 'The deprivation of food can take many forms and have quite disparate causes as well as distinct effects', and empowering women could lead to a large number of social and economic benefits, which in turn could effectively address malnutrition issues.[30]

It is therefore essential that a new administrative approach is taken to achieve policy objectives, if the population growth rate is to be brought down. The approach needs to be holistic as suggested by Nair, but equally important is getting people involved at the grass root level. With peoples' genuine involvement miracles can be achieved. There are plenty of lessons in history which provides proof of this—not too long ago Vietnam achieved the unthinkable by winning the war against the mightiest military power on earth. There cannot be a better example than this in demonstrating the importance of getting people involved in attaining policy and program objectives.

However, attempts to obtain genuine grass root participation must avoid any tokenism. Often it is found that powerful segments in the community cleverly use their position simply by advising the community of certain actions and use this as proxy for participation. This process may succeed initially, but in the long run this could lead to loss of faith in the consultation process by the community (Bhatt 1997:371–86). Should this happen, peoples' mistrust in the governance process will harden and any future attempts to get people genuinely involved in a consultation process will be suspiciously interpreted by the community.

IIIB Human Resources

There is a saying that two economists hardly ever agree on economic issues. While this may be true in majority of circumstances, on one issue economists tend to agree; that the development of human resources is an essential precondition for achieving a sustained level of development. This is becoming a key element in international development cooperation program as well (Elek 1997). Multilateral

---

29 smail, R.S., (1997), Head UNICEF Information Service, India in a Press interview, The *Economic Times*, New Delhi, 23 December.

30 Sen, Professor A.K., (1997). Hunger can't end by just more food, Inaugural Lecture of the Rajendra Prasad Memorial Lecture Series, New Delhi, 11 June.

development agencies and regional organisations are all focussing on this aspect along with a focus on community building.

The UNDP identifies six essential actions required to eradicate poverty in the 21st century (UNDP 1997:106–16). Two of these essential actions are

- empowering individuals, households and communities to gain greater control over their life; and
- strengthening gender equality to empower women release their vast under used energy and creativity. Poverty eradication without gender equality is impossible, and a contradiction in terms.

Within this context, India's performance has been poor. Nearly 49 per cent of its adult population is illiterate, public investment on social infrastructure has been declining, and the economic and decision making powers are concentrated in few hands or privileged groups in spite of a democratic form of government.

Extreme poverty also debars at least one third of the Indian population from effectively participating in social, economic and political activities, and thus denies them a voice to express and analyse their problems and priorities. Experience from other developing countries indicates that through participation and empowerment a deprived community (particularly the poor) can effectively challenge the perceptions of those in authority and begin to change attitudes and agendas (UNDP 1997:106–16).

In spite of these deficiencies, total expenditure on education as a percentage of GNP has remained comparatively small. In 1960 it was 2.3 per cent, in 1980 it was 2.8 per cent and in 1993–94 it increased to 3.8 per cent only (UNDP 1990; 1997:181). However, the proportion of central government expenditure on education has remained same during last 15 years in spite of the urgent priority this sector requires. In 1980, 1.9 per cent of central government expenditure was directed to the education sector, and the percentage has remained same during the period 1992–95 (UNDP 1997). The policy failures in this sector can be also seen from the unusual structure of the Indian education system.

For a country where such a large number of the adult population is illiterate, there are 197 universities and 34 deemed universities (i.e. university status) with a teacher population of about 287,000 (Basu 1997). This sector is funded entirely from the public exchequer. Tuition fees for courses are a few cents per head per month, or a maximum of few dollars a year. Naturally, this has created an unbalanced education structure which has neglected the primary sector, the basis of any worthwhile public education policy. As Basu states: 'For most countries, the [education] house will look like a pyramid, tapering off rapidly as one goes higher up. In the case of India, the building is more like a tower.'

While Basu rightly points out the absurdity of India's education policy, his suggestion that the higher education sector be left to market forces needs debating within the community. If it is left to market forces alone, people with merit but without resources may not get access to higher education. Education policy must ensure that merit remains the focus of higher education, although some restrictions may be required. Significant focus on restructuring university courses, and large expansion in the technical and vocational education area is required if higher education restriction policies are to be successful. This point is raised because the social and economic divisions between élite and non-élite classes in India in many ways is very pronounced. If higher education is left to market forces alone, another underprivileged class will be created who will be forced by circumstances to remain subservient to those able to buy higher education irrespective of merit.

It is also well established that good quality primary education provides a sound base for technological efficiency. Professor Little's study of the successes of the Taiwan and South Korean economies found that the high quality of their primary education has been one of the main reasons for their rapid industrial growth in high technology areas (Bhagwati 1996:9). Furthermore, with the globalisation of national economies the importance of good quality primary education within a nations' economic structure assumes added significance as increasingly industrial structure will undergo rapid changes in favour of technology dominated structure. If the labour force is not trained and geared to face this challenge, they will remain poverty trapped in perpetuity. For example, following the massive restructuring of the New Zealand economy, for the first time in its history it lost more island population in the early 1990s than it gained from its island territories (Appleyard and Stahl 1995:16–9). Almost 100 per cent of the island workers were employed in jobs which required virtually no formal education, and with the restructuring they found that their jobs had disappeared forever.

Besides its economic consequences, the failure to provide primary education has resulted in a large section of India's population not being adequately empowered to occupy their rightful place in society, in the decision making process of the government. As a result while they remained entitled to vote in elections, the effectiveness of their vote remains somewhat diminished as they collectively remain prone to pressures from elements in society who want them to remain less empowered.

In spite of its large numbers, India's human resources remain undeveloped. In addition to its economic consequences, the social and political consequences of such failures are enormous. If a large number of the population is kept behind, a time is bound to come when the deprived people feel the importance of not having any stake in the nation's development and welfare creating fertile ground for disruptive forces. Empowering people to become a part of the society is the best way to ensure progress and peace, as well as creating a momentum whereby the economy can readjust itself within a continuously changing economic environment. This situation is widely acknowledged by development economists, who are concerned that globalisation of national economies will not bring benefits to the majority of the population unless sectors such as basic education and elementary health care are given priority in governments' policies. In a recent speech in India Amartya Sen, a well known development economist, bluntly put it the reform initiatives in India are lopsided. He further attributed the success of China's contemporary market-based economic success on the solid foundation of social changes that had occurred earlier. If India is to achieve this success, it has to prepare the foundations first.[31]

To develop a strong human-resource base, coordinated policy initiative is required incorporating three areas, primary education, vocational and technical education and tertiary education. Even developed countries that can afford to sustain a large tertiary sector are critically examining the entire education sector within the rapidly changing economic and technological environment.

In India's case the task is complex because it has a very poor structural base in the primary education sector and almost one half of its entire adult population needs to be brought within the primary education sector's net. This is a far more complex task than providing primary

---

31 Sen, A. (1997). In a speech at the Confederation of Indian Industries (CCII) in New Delhi on 29 November. A summary of the speech was published in most of the Indian dailies on 30 November.

education to children. In the former case social and economic issues will influence their participation in any program to build their capacity to absorb new technology and idea for their vocation. Policy framers need to clearly understand and recognise India's cultural and behavioural diversity before developing human resource development policies. In particular, adult education, technical and vocational education policies and strategies cannot ignore the stark realities of economic and social conditions, values and strengths, which influence the adult population more than the primary-age group population. A holistic and pragmatic approach is required to develop India's human resources, and the temptation to blindly follow the policies of other countries should be avoided.

IIIC Energy

Assurance of an uninterrupted energy supply at a competitive price is one of the essential infrastructure factors investors consider before making their investment decisions. Energy was one of the key bottlenecks in the past and remains a major impediment to increased industrial and commercial investments in India.

Investment in the energy sector has been virtually monopolised by the public sector until very recently. Following the decision to open up the economy for competition during the eighth plan period (1992–97), this sector was opened to private sector including international investment. To encourage investment, the government initiated institutional reforms, which are considered vital for the growth of this sector. States which have primary responsibility for the energy sector have also started taking initiatives to overhaul its management. This has resulted in increasing private sector investment in the energy sector.

Apart from supply constraints, the inefficient use of energy by many industries with outdated production techniques and machinery, inappropriate pricing policy, high percentage of loss in power transmission, and large scale power theft remain major concerns for the management of the energy sector. Many of these concerns are technical and operational in nature. Energy pricing policy also remains a politically sensitive issue and it will require firm leadership from governments at various levels.

India's per capita energy consumption of nine gigajoules was one of the lowest in the beginning of this decade when compared with other countries such as Australia's 215, Singapore's 171 and China's 23.

Energy consumption will increase significantly in the coming decades, but the rate of increase will be accelerated compared to previous increases. In 1994, per capita commercial energy consumption was 243 kilograms of oil equivalent compared to 112 kilograms in 1971. The average annual per capita increase was 5.86 kg between 1971 and 1992, whereas the average between 1980–94 period was 7.57 kg (World Bank 1994b:170–1).

Table 10: Ratio of per capita energy consumption (oil equivalent) and contribution to GDP

	P/capita oil equivalent energy consumption		% change 1980–94.	Contribution to GDP per kg oil consumption (US$ in 1987 prices)		% change 1980–94.
	1980	1994		1980	1994	
Australia	4,792	5,173	8.0	2.3	3.6	56.5
China	421	647	54.0	0.5	0.7	40.0
Indonesia	169	393	133.0	3.1	2.3	–25.8
India	137	243	77.0	1.8	1.3	-27.8

Source: World Bank 1996. *World Development Report*, World Bank, Washington, DC.

This table clearly shows that India's energy consumption is not only low in comparison to developed countries such as Australia, but more significantly it is low compared to China and Indonesia. Currently India imports a significant amount of energy resources at a huge foreign exchange cost. As the industrialisation and urbanisation momentum increases, the rate of increase in consumption will also accelerate. The increased demand has to be met either by increasing domestic energy sources or by increasing imports in conjunction with increased efficiency in production, distribution and consumption. In this regard India is slipping backwards like Indonesia. In 1994 contribution to GDP by each kilogram of oil consumption declined by more than one quarter of one percentage point, which compares very unfavourably with both Australia and China. While in Australia's case one can argue that it is a developed country and it has initiated major structural changes in both the production and distribution of power and hence the outcome is not totally unexpected. A comparison with China's is much more relevant; it clearly shows that while China is increasingly becoming efficient in energy use, India is becoming inefficient in terms of its contribution to the gross domestic product.

Installed power generation capacity currently stands at 83,287 MW of which 72 per cent is thermal (includes a small amount from non-conventional sources), 25 per cent hydro and 3 per cent nuclear (Government of India 1997:374–95). During last few years approval has been given for a number of new power stations on completion of which the installed capacity will increase significantly.

India's known coal, oil and gas reserves are small compared to its requirements. Its known coal reserve is about 131,300 million metric tons of which about 48 per cent are proven recoverable reserve. It has a proven recoverable crude oil reserve of 810 million metric tons and 730 billion cubic meters of natural gas (World Resources 1994:336–7). When these reserves are considered against its huge population and rising demand, the energy stock is small.

By contrast however, India's potential hydroelectric generating capacity is one of the highest in the world, estimated to be in the range of 205,000 megawatts. Only 10 other countries and the former Soviet Union have a higher hydroelectric generating potential than India. In the region, both China and Indonesia have a higher potential than India. Nepal, India's neighbour has also a significant capacity, although it is less than India's. Currently India has an installed capacity of only about 18,900 megawatts—about nine per cent of its estimated potential.

However, there are a number of hurdles before power can be harnessed from this source. First and foremost is the large capital requirement to build dams and power stations. Secondly, the damming of rivers in India will require cross national boundary cooperation as in a number of cases they flow through more than one country. Thirdly, given the high population density in India construction of dams will require uprooting a large number of people who do not have any alternative livelihood other than agriculture. Fourthly, environmental and ecological issues are also increasingly becoming a concern to the population. The non-government sector in India is not only articulating the reasons for their concern, but they have also shown a resilient capacity to internationalise their concerns in collaboration with international non-government agencies working in the environment field. If past experience is any guide, their capacity to raise public concern both nationally and globally should not be underestimated.

Finally, indifferent management practices in dealing with people uprooted from dam construction sites are increasingly reinforcing opposition to proposals for hydroelectric schemes by affected communities and non-government organisations. It is an issue which governments have failed time and again to address adequately and efficiently. Governments' failures have hardened the resolve of residents and non-government organisations to oppose construction of dams by uprooting people from the land required for construction work. One such recent example is the Bargi Dam oustees. In spite of significant agitation and promises at the highest level, the ousted people are yet to receive the benefits such as drinking water or a health centre in their new location a decade later.[32]

Two other important sources of energy are nuclear power and the sun. India already has a number of nuclear power stations. If press reports are any guide the safety record of India's nuclear power stations is not very good. Nuclear power stations are also very capital intensive and require meticulous maintenance. In general, the record of industrial maintenance in India can be classified as poor to patchy. Although solar energy has significant potential, it has not yet become economic when compared to other available sources. With improvements in the harnessing technology, it could be an important, pollution free source. At this stage it is not considered a major source although its potential remains enormous. Some coastal areas use wind generated power, but its full potential has not yet been fully realised.

Assuming that the current per capita annual consumption will reach 9 kg of oil equivalent in 2010—a very conservative estimate compared to the average consumption of 7.57 kg of oil equivalent during the 1980–94 period—India's energy consumption will be between 10.5 and 11 billion kg of oil equivalent (based on population growth rate under three alternative growth assumptions). Assuming per capita annual consumption to reach oil equivalent of 11 kg, an increase of 2 kg per capita to the year 2025, India's annual energy requirement will be between 14 and 16.5 billion kg oil equivalent in 2025.

The important question is can India afford to maintain the level of energy imports as domestic supply from the known sources will be inadequate to satisfy this demand? Although in 1993 the proportion of the value of fuel import to total import declined to 30 per cent from 45

---

32 *Statesman Weekly*, 1997. 'Bargi Dam oustees live a 'life of animals', Calcutta, 30 August.

per cent in 1980, the fuel sector will have to compete for foreign exchange with other sectors as the economy picks up. In this context it is worth noting that in 1992, 26 per cent of the income equivalent from merchandise exports was paid to cover the costs of energy import. In 1971 the payment was only 12 per cent of the income equivalent from merchandise export (World Bank 1994b:170–1).

Table 11: Growth of merchandise export and fuel import during 1986–95 (US$ million)

Items/fiscal year	1986	1990	1993	1995	Changes 1986–95
Merchandise exports (ME)	10,420	18,477	22,683	32,433	+211 %
as a per centage of GDP	4.5	6.2	8.8	9.9	
Total imports (TP)	17,740	27,914	25,069	41,721	+135 %
as a per centage of GDP	7.7	9.4	9.7	12.7	
Fuel import as a per centage of ME in value terms	21.0	32.5	24.9	22.2	

Source: World Bank (India) 1997. *Economic Update: sustaining rapid growth*, World Bank Washington, DC.

Besides the high cost of importing fuel, uninterrupted guaranteed supply of fuel also remains a concern. Globally, oil is always linked with political intrigue and drama. Thus it is absolutely essential to look at this issue from political side as well, otherwise in a politically uncertain environment the supply of oil could be used as a weapon to damage the economy. India has been politically active to ensure a steady and uninterrupted supply of oil. Informed sources confirm that the Government has achieved only limited success. Initially an attempt was made to import gas and oil from Oman through an undersea pipeline in the Arabian Sea to the west coast of India. This did not materialise. A proposal to import from Turkmenistan through a land-based pipeline also did not materialise because of the political situation in Afganisthan, through which the pipeline was to be laid. A proposal to import from Iran via Pakistan did not progress either, also believed to be for political reasons.

Gas reserves estimated to last until 2025 have been discovered in Bangladesh. The government there has indicated that it is actively considering gas export to India via a pipeline. If this comes to fruition it would ease India's energy concerns for about a decade.[33] The recent move by the Indian Oil and Natural Gas Corporation (ONGC) to finalise an agreement with its Chinese counterpart to share production and distribution of oil and gas from Kazakisthan appears promising. Kazakisthan is believed to have unlimited reserves. Given India and China's desire to achieve rapid economic growth any agreement to ensure energy supply to both these countries will assist in diffusing political tension as well.

Energy being such a vital sector, it would be inappropriate to look at this issue from the supply side alone. A strong case exists to look at this issue from the demand-side and cost recovery angles as well. Past experience has shown the power of the organised road transport sector to bring the economy to its knees when the government wanted to recover some part of the actual costs from the road transport sector. Increasing car ownership in India, particularly by the middle-class will also create policy pressures to favour the politically articulate and powerful upper middle class population which has the capacity to seek policy advantages for themselves.

Notwithstanding the above, a comprehensive demand-side policy is urgently required if the serious consequences of shortage in supply are to be avoided in the next decades. Some of the important issues which require urgent consideration are: road tax, excise on fuel, time differential pricing policies to even-out commercial, industrial and domestic demands during a twenty-four hour period to avoid the need for substantial stand-by extra generating capacity to meet peak demands, and parking policies in urban centres. Better coordination between the hydro and thermal power generating sectors may reduce the necessity to keep large stand-by generating capacity to meet peak demands because the quantity of hydro-electric generated power can be easily adjusted with marginal increase in running costs.

---

33 Huq, E., 1998. 'Bangladesh considering natural gas export to India', *Economic Times*, New Delhi, 24 March.

Chapter Three: Governance Issues

I Good Governance in India: Peoples' Perception

In India's 50th year of independence in 1997, the national weekly *India Today* commissioned a nation-wide poll to establish the nation's mood on a number of critical issues.[34] The results of this survey indicate that good governance or civil society related issues remain a major concern of the population at large. The survey found that

- 47 per cent believed that India will disintegrate in 50 years
- 43 per cent believed that the present law and order situation is worse than under the British
- 55 per cent believed that politicians are dishonest, 6 per cent believe them to be honest
- 60 per cent believed police are dishonest, 7 per cent believe them to be honest
- 51 per cent believed that 51 per cent of their parliamentary representatives are not at all interested in solving the problems of their constituency.[35]

On the question of which issues are the greatest threat to the country

- 34 per cent identified corruption as biggest evil followed by unemployment (20 per cent) and rising prices (18 per cent).

These responses unequivocally show the people's lack of confidence in the political process, politicians, police, administration and in those who are in positions of power or authority. The results also confirm the sentiments expressed in numerous letters to the editor. For example, one metropolitan daily published 15 letters three days before the independence day celebrations in 1997 of which 12 letters, (a staggering 75 per cent) expressed serious reservations about the state of the country and its achievements during 50 years of independence.[36] The themes of letters published in other metropolitan dailies varied, but similar sentiments dominated.

---

34 *India Today,* 1947–97, Special Issue (1997). 'India: State of the Nation', New Delhi:42–53.

35 Don't know/can't say respondants are proportionately distributed to those who responded.

36 *Bartaman* (Metropolitan daily), 1997, Calcutta, 12 August.

To find out the reasons for peoples' loss of faith in the governance process it is essential to carefully examine complex issues such as intra and inter-relationship between the state, government and the community. In such an examination value judgements are unavoidable. In India's case a significant amount of anecdotal evidence is available which confirms that the perception of people as reflected in the survey results are justified.

Any examination of the performance of a government must acknowledge the differing perspectives of different sections of the community. Communities within a nation play a collective role to ensure and enhance national interest, and they also play a role to enhance their own individual sectional interests. The community's role as a preserver and promoter of sectional interest needs to be understood and accommodated within the national goals and objectives to minimise chances of conflict. It is therefore essential to understand the aspirations, as well as the roles of each of these individual communities in the development of a nation and in the promotion of good governance practices. Besides the community at large, institutions such as political parties, government, bureaucracy, the judiciary and non-government organisations also individually and collectively contribute, through their actions, to the promotion and nurturing of good governance practices and healthy constitutional conventions.

The Indian Constitution guarantees fundamental rights to its citizens—civil, political and legal in nature. None of these fundamental rights incorporate economic rights. The social and economic rights are incorporated in the *Directive Principles of State Policy* (DPSP), which is a unique feature of the Indian Constitution. Rights incorporated in this category cannot be legally enforced (Mukherjee and Mukherjee 1995:91–9).

Constitutional rights effectively remain out of bounds to communities without education and those were living in a poverty-stricken environment. Such communities can neither understand nor use their immense power effectively to elect and unseat governments, as is their right, enshrined in the Constitution. A recent press report which vividly describes the magnitude of poverty in a large district and how the people will vote in the national election confirms this situation.[37]

37 Mohanti, S., 1998. 'Ballots on sale. For the hungry also vote', *The Economic Times*, New Delhi, 21 February.

In 1995 the adult illiteracy rate in India was nearly 49 per cent—35 per cent of males and 62 per cent of females; per capita gross national product (GNP) was $340; and 53 per cent of the population were living on less than one dollar a day (World Bank 1997:214), and 35 per cent of the total population were living below the poverty line. Twenty per cent of the population had five times more real GDP per capita during 1980–94 compared with the poorest 20 per cent (UNDP 1997:53–5). Rural poverty is endemic: of the 313 million people living below the poverty line 241 million (74 per cent) live in rural areas. The incidence of poverty was 68 per cent amongst landless wage earners, 51 per cent amongst scheduled castes and scheduled tribes, and 45 per cent amongst households in which no-one was literate (World Bank 1997b).

This high illiteracy rate and the inability of a very significant proportion of the population to enjoy a basic standard of living impinged on the community's capacity to either directly contribute or adhere to primacy of good governance principles. In such situations the disadvantaged and dispossessed people cannot feel empowered and become the group most vulnerable to exploitation by the economically and socially powerful groups keen to perpetuate their privileged and dominant positions within the community. Furthermore, poverty and illiteracy draws people to violate the norms of a civil society, often without them knowing or understanding the consequences of the activities they were engaged to undertake by the vested interest. In this environment money and anti-social elements, backed by unscrupulous politicians, in many cases dominate elections.

India's Election Commission publicly asserted that all large political parties in India were harbouring and using anti-social elements in political activities and elections.[38] Even though the Commission is trying to stop criminal elements taking part in elections and governments, it has not achieved much success. For example, 16 members of the 93 member Cabinet in the State of Uttar Pradesh in 1997 (Kalyan Singh Ministry) have been accused of serious crimes, as

38 Gill, M.S., 1997. Chief Election Commissioner at a Press Conference 18 August, Calcutta. All major dailies in India reported this in their next day edition.

have nearly one third of the members of the state legislature.[39] A somewhat similar situation can be found in other states as well.

A major constraint to encouraging and promoting good governance practices in India was the complete non-existence of any separation of powers between the government and administration. In most countries where Westminster tradition is followed, a clear distinction exists between policy makers (government) and the executors of those policies (bureaucracy). This system clearly identifies administrative responsibilities where bureaucracy can perform their assigned tasks without fear or favour, and without interference by the government. In India some ministers often at junior levels are directly involved in granting permits, licenses and interfere in the posting and transfer of officers. This provides a fertile ground for corrupt nexus between politicians and bureaucrats. Once the distinction between the government and the bureaucracy becomes invisible or blurred, the bureaucracy tends to toe the line of their political masters irrespective of what they are supposed to do.

Political masters in an unscrupulous environment also take the opportunity to fully use the bureaucracy to satisfy their own political and personal agenda. The power most abused by governments, to ensure that bureaucracy remains subordinate to their whims and not to the laws and regulations of the country, is the power to transfer officials, even senior ones, without assigning any reason, almost totally at their will. To avoid such harassment, many, except officers with the highest integrity, find it easier to follow the wishes of their political masters and protect their self-interest in an environment where alternative employment opportunities are relatively few, and postings outside capital cities do not provide many of the modern day living facilities. The World Bank rightly opined that in India senior civil servants are transferred frequently, and estimated that the average tenure of field officers can be as low as eight months which significantly contributed in the decline and effectiveness of the service (World Bank 1997:93–4). A classic example of this situation was recently observed in the state of Bihar when five senior officials (one after another) were

---

39 Goldenburg, S., 1998. 'Indian election marred by violent rivalry', reporting for the *Guardian*, London; reprinted in the *Canberra Times*, 10 February.

appointed to take charge of the Inspector General of Prisons within 45 days.[40]

II Constitutional Provisions: Have These Been Followed Scrupulously?

India is a federal country with three layers of government: central, state and local. Power sharing arrangements between these three levels of governments are not similar to those found in most other federations. Indian federation was not constituted by any agreement between constituent units, and states have no right to secede. The central government in India wields vast powers via its regulation of commerce and industry and the distribution of revenues between the Union and States. It also has the power to dismiss elected state governments by imposing President's Rule under article 356 of the Constitution (Parthasarathy 1996).

This makes the relationship between the centre and states unequal with the centre having virtually unlimited legal power to subvert elected state governments by citing constitutional grounds, should it so desire. The relationship between other two levels of government (state and local government) is no better, although the specific focus on the implementation of the Panchayeti system has the potential to improve this relationship if the principles are followed scrupulously and education, training and resources are provided. The failure to follow a cooperative principle of sharing power and strictly adhere to the spirit of the constitutional provisions have contributed significantly to the violation of good governance principles and practices.

The Central Government appoints Governors, some of whom have often acted to please their appointing authority by providing reports which would justify the declaration of President's rule and the dismissal of an elected state government by the Central Government. Regrettably, central governments of all political persuasions often use, or threatened to use, this discretionary constitutional power to resolve their intra-party leadership difficulties or to dismiss opposition led state governments. Although the Supreme Court has put some clarifications on the indiscriminate use of this article from time to time, in reality the entire issue remains confused, particularly with the contradiction

---

40 *The Statesman,* 1997. 'Bihar's fifth I-G (prisons) in 45 days', Calcutta, 19 August.

between clauses (1) and (2) of Article 163. Within this context Governors' power under clause 356 will remain confused, and there is no guarantee that this power will not be misused (Chaube 1997). The entire issue of the President's power to dismiss a democratically elected state government on the basis of a Governor's report needs to be examined more thoroughly than has been done to date.

This problem began within 18 months of the promulgation of the Indian Constitution in January 1950. Dr G.C. Bhargava, the then Congress Chief Minister of the province of Punjab was asked by the Congress Parliamentary Board to resign although he had a majority in the Legislative Assembly in June 1951. In his resignation letter he bluntly stated that he was resigning on the orders of the Congress Parliamentary Board. At this the then President (Rajendra Prasad) told the Prime Minister (Nehru) that by this action the Government was taking away the powers from the representative of the people to hand them over to the bureaucrats (Noorani 1989).

Another instance of a violation of the spirit of the Constitution at an early stage in its life was the nomination of the late Rajagopalachari, a Congress Party member, to the Legislative Council by the Governor of Madras (Tamilnadu) in March 1952. He later asked Rajagopalachari to form a government even though a general election had already taken place and a government was shortly to be installed. The Governor's decision was challenged at the High Court which refused to adjudicate on technical grounds (Chatterjee 1997). The High Court, however, rightly refused to rule on the political issue raised by the applicant that a member of the Legislative Council could not be nominated for the position of Chief Minister. These violations at an early stage in the life of the new constitution did not contribute to the growth of healthy constitutional practice and tradition. Constitutional conventions and political traditions are essential elements for a smoothly functioning democratic society.

This turn around within 18 months of the promulgation of the constitution could perhaps be seen as the beginning of the constitutional decaying process which has culminated in the current situation. However, so long was the same party in power both at the central and state levels that the dismissal of elected state governments on questionable grounds was politically manageable, though morally unjustified and an indefensible political practice.

The situation took a different turn when for the first time in the Indian political history a government of different political persuasion was elected in the state of Kerala in 1957. However, political unrest in the state was fuelled or at least encouraged by the vested interest groups who felt threatened by some government policies. They in alliance with communal and other forces started agitation and many of the government's programs could not be implemented, and in some instances the normal functioning of the government could not be carried out. The then Prime Minister publicly said that he was not in favour of dismissing the government. The President of the ruling party at the centre however met the President on 25 July 1959 and then publicly declared that central government action was long overdue in view of the hard facts of the situation. Soon after the state government was dismissed (Noorani 1984a).

During the drafting stage of the constitution the Chairman of the drafting committee and senior leaders categorically stated first, that the imposition of President's rule should be only in extreme circumstances—whether there was good government or not in the province was not for the Centre to determine—and second, the appointed governors must be acceptable to the states. There have been regular violations of these two important undertakings over the last four decades. It should, however, be stressed that the situation in many instances was assisted by inept political leadership and unprincipled shifting of allegiance in legislatures by elected representatives to obtain personal gains. On the issue of appointment of Governors in States, at least two non-Congress state Chief Ministers publicly stated that they were not consulted when Governors in their states were appointed (Noorani 1984b).

It is only the first time in history that in 1997 the President demonstrated his inclination to promote a healthy convention by asking the Cabinet to reconsider its recommendation to impose President's rule in the state of Uttar Pradesh although the State Government enjoyed majority in the Legislature. The role of the Uttar Pradesh Governor in recommending President's rule has been, to say the least, dubious. The Cabinet, for its part, by not reasserting that President's rule should be imposed assisted the President in contributing to the development of a healthy convention, that so long the government enjoys legislature's confidence and there is no major law and order breakdown in the state, Article 356 should not be promulgated.

The growth of powerful central institutions such as the Planning Commission, which decides state development expenditure and influences the location of industries, also contributed to the development of an unhealthy political convention. This prompted many constitutional experts and state leaders to seek a review of the existing administrative and constitutional arrangements, particularly with respect to the centre-state relationship. The pressure gained momentum when a number of state treasury benches were occupied by a political party other than the party in power at the Centre, particularly during the 1970s. Eventually a judicial commission headed by a retired Supreme Court Justice (R.S. Sarkaria) was appointed to examine this relationship issue in 1980.

Justice Sarkaria submitted his report in 1988 which contained some 250 recommendations, and it received its fair share of bouquets along with criticisms for not recommending any fundamental changes in the central-state administrative arrangements (Sarkaria 1988). Irrespective of its alleged shortcomings, its considerable emphasis on the need for healthy political conventions to promote the principle of cooperative federalism; its criticism of the abuse of Article 356 of the Constitution for political interest, and hence the need to develop a benchmark in this area, are two of his most important recommendations. Political scientists and federal-state relationship experts in India acknowledge that federalism and pluralism are two essential principles for organising heterogeneous societies into a viable share of political power sharing by reconciling the twin purposes of political unification and diversity (Kidwai 1997). Although nearly a decade has passed since the Sarkaria report was produced, the country has yet to develop a healthy convention on the federal-state relationship.

III Political Parties

In pre-independence days Congress was the dominant political party and its respected leadership attracted people to its fold. At that time Congress identified itself with the independence movement and peoples' support was overwhelming. The single objective of gaining independence overshadowed other important policy issues during this period. Besides Gandhi, who was considered more a saint by the masses, not a political leader *per se*, party leadership was dominated by people from the comparatively well-off class. On gaining independence the political agenda changed and without the towering personality of a saintly figure such as Gandhi as undisputed leader of the party, some powerful sections of the well-off class started to influence the operation of the government in a way which would disproportionately benefit them.

The unchallenged power enjoyed by the Congress Party in the post-independence period, its questionable use of constitutional provisions and the leadership's failure to prevent undesirable elements using the party for private gains at the cost of the community, only hastened the erosion of its mass base over the years. These are some of the important reasons amongst many why, in spite of its rhetoric, many of the strong people focus policies (with a socialist ring) were generally little more than vote-catching rhetoric (Brown 1997:22–7).

Notwithstanding these failures, based on its pre-independence record and continuation of its pre-independence leadership of Nehru, followed by his daughter, Congress continued to enjoy popular support all over the country. During this period, opposition leaders failed to make any substantial dent in the power base of Congress which gave the impression of championing the causes of minorities and backward communities. Within this context Kohli's observation that powerful leaders often proved to be enemies of institutions such as political parties certainly proves to be valid in post-independent India (Kohli 1992:402).

However, the decline of Congress in the post-Nehru Indira Gandhi period was not matched by a rise by other national political parties. As secular political parties failed to establish an all-India base to fill the vacuum created by the decline of Congress, single-issue based linguistic, religious and ethnic regional parties quickly filled it. This has created an environment of political uncertainty at the federal level, although at provincial levels these parties have gradually reinforced their bases, further setting back the emergence of a truly national party to emerge. A lack of charismatic national leadership is indeed one important reason, but more importantly political parties are themselves to blame for not being able to secure peoples' confidence at the national level.

Many of the Indian political parties have not only failed to provide leadership, they also have failed to observe democratic principles in administering their parties. The old saying that if a party cannot organise its affairs democratically, how could it rule the country democratically sounds very prophetic in India's case. Congress, once the largest mass-based party, has shunned internal democracy by concentrating power in the hands of its High Command with a focus on dynastic leadership during last few decades. Even as recently as in 1998, following its defeat in the general election, it reverted to a dynastic leader who replaced an elected president. The specific point in contention here is that an elected president was replaced by a person who did not come through any election process and only recently became a card carrying member of the party. This again signals that the views of the ordinary membership does not matter so long one has the right connections. Such practices neither assist the party, nor democratic political processes to flourish. They have become widespread, as many parties are based on the narrow self-interests of locally based powerful individuals or *kulaks* or political *satraps*.

Such practices encourage authoritarian tendencies to grow and flourish. In 1997 the Election Commission threatened to withdraw its recognition of a regional party which refused to hold an election to elect party office bearers. The said party put one individual as its president for life which was unacceptable to the Commission. The party reluctantly agreed to accept the Commission's direction with the proviso that it would take time to modify its constitution to give effect to the Commission's directives.[41]

In addition to their failure to democratise their organisational structures, political parties have also often failed to properly account for their income and expenditure. This failure creates an environment fertile for corrupt practices and encourages an unsavoury relationship with financially powerful groups and anti-social elements. Stringent enforcement of financial accountability is required to ensure that political parties do not become agents for those who can afford to influence government policies by contributing to their funds without public knowledge or scrutiny. Furthermore, in an environment where national economies are becoming an integral part of the global economy, the scope for unduly influencing policies of sovereign governments by controlling a political party's policy making power through financial contributions remain a real possibility. Dictators in a number of countries in the past received such contributions, which eventually ended up in secret foreign bank accounts.

---

41 The *Statesman Weekly*, 1998. 'Sena wards for derecognition threat with a vow to amend constitution', Calcutta, 3 January.

The Indian situation does not compare favourably with practices followed in other democratic countries where Westminster principles are followed and practiced. For example, in America even the President and Vice-President are not spared from investigation by law enforcement agencies seeking detailed information on fund raising activities to ensure that they did not break any law.[42] Similarly, the Blair government in the United Kingdom in 1997 was forced to declare that it would return all contributions received from a tobacco company as it could compromise its position on the tobacco sponsorship of sports. Contrary to these well established practices, Indian political parties try their best not to divulge the source of their income. An example is the government's investigation of a foreign donation to the Congress party which earned it a sharp rebuke from the Delhi High Court.

In many cases political leadership made noises, but failed to act when they got the opportunity to put their policies into practice to overcome the perceived deficiencies in the political process. For example, at the special four-day session of the Indian Parliament to mark Golden Jubilee of India's independence, Parliamentarians identified corruption and criminalisation of politics as the biggest problem facing the country. They also acknowledged that an overactive judiciary would not solve these problems; it would create distortions.[43] Yet, when called for action they failed to prescribe measures which would make it unnecessary for the judiciary to interfere in functions which are normally expected from the legislature and executive.

The 1996 general election was universally regarded as the cleanest and fairest election in the history of the country. The recent attempt to raise the powers of the Election Commission to develop and administer a well-defined model code for political parties was opposed by virtually all political parties. The draft code attempted to ensure that assessment of the practices of political parties (which were somewhat arbitrarily addressed by the Commission in 1996) to ensure a free and fair election does not have to remain arbitrary. Many political parties did not like this strict enforcement of election rules. It is no wonder that most of

---

42 Kettle, M., 1997. 'Clinton and Gore quizzed by FBI over party funds', reporting for the *Guardian*, London; quoted in the *Canberra Times*, Canberra, 14 November.

43 The *Statesman Weekly*, 1997. 'Corruption biggest menace, say MPs', Calcutta, 6 September.

the political parties opposed this reform measure and considered the actions of the Commission in 1996 high-handed.[44]

A further failure of these political parties is their incapacity to match their activities with their declared policies. For example, each of the political parties declare their allegiance to the democratic form of government and to the Indian Constitution. However, when they are out of power, they themselves do not hesitate to take recourse to undemocratic methods to pursue their point of view or champion their cause. The indiscriminate use of the weapon of general strike, popularly known as *bandh,* is an example. Again, their indiscriminate call to citizens to violate the law to demonstrate their opposition (known as Satyagraha, championed by Gandhi during the independence movement) to governments' policies creates a psychology of defiance which does not help promote good governance practices or a civil society. Activities which are acceptable in the independence movement context may be totally unacceptable in a democratic form of government, which is owned by citizens themselves.

The call by some political parties to violate laws and regulations to promote their cause is often justified on the grounds that the party concerned could not find any other way to convey their political point. This is a method that was extensively pursued in the pre-independence days when the call for non-cooperation and disobeyance of the law of the country was impeccably backed by the moral authority of the political leadership. The post-independent leadership could not provide such moral authority and leadership. Also, it should be acknowledged that in the changed political environment it becomes a difficult issue as the political enemy is no longer a colonial power. Therefore, the call to violate country's laws as a potent political weapon does not carry with it the moral justification it did in pre-independence days. Yet, the political parties remain unperturbed while using this weapon in the contemporary political environment.

When civil society laws and practices are violated to serve sectional or minority interests and fail to attract popular support, people tend to remain passive spectators by not actively opposing such activities. For example, many people do not support *bandh* as it has lost its potency, but they do not want to be identified by opposing a *bandh* lest they

---

44 Kumar, P., 1997. 'Politicians insists bill should curb poll panel clout', *The Asian Age*, Calcutta, 31 July.

might have to face harassment and even physical harm. *Bandhs* at the same time adversely affect workers in the unorganised sector, which dominates the Indian economy.

On a public interest application the Kerala High Court declared *bandh* unconstitutional and argued that no political party or any other agency should have the right to stop industry or business functioning or deny the basic rights of a citizen to work by calling *bandh*. As the success of *bandhs* in recent years was mainly due to direct and indirect compulsion applied by organisers, the court was right in its judgement (Mukhopadhaya 1997). It is a disappointing reflection on Indian political parties that a powerful political weapon such as *bandh* has become a judicial issue due to their indiscretion.

IV Indian Bureaucracy

On becoming a sovereign democratic republic in 1950, India essentially maintained its Westminster modeled administrative structure. In that structure bureaucracy plays a vital role in translating government policies into actions. It also gives practical shape to the constitutional provisions, contributes in institution building relevant to the progress of individuals and the community. The system of recruitment as practiced in India is loosely known as the mandarin system, whereby employees are hired into a career stream or corps rather than for specific jobs. Under this system recruitment is centralised through a rigorous entrance examination and normally maintains age restrictions for entry (World Bank 1997a:94).

Following selection recruits are given one year's managerial training before their positions are assigned—usually at the block development level. Vertical mobility is virtually assured to the highest level of bureaucracy. Although competition remains high for entry to the administrative service, the recruitment system fails to draw from a significant proportion of the population. When only a small, privileged class gets the opportunity to pursue higher education, this limited scope to enter the civil service through one entry point does not ensure participation from all socioeconomic sections of the community, and also cannot assure that those recruited through this process are capable of adopting innovative practices in public administration, demonstrating leadership and commitment to serve the entire community and not just their own privileged section.

Parallel to the administrative service recruitment, the government has also commenced recruitment along similar lines for specific services such as the forestry service and economic service. However, they also suffer from the same drawback—only a small section of the community can take advantage of this recruitment process and a significant number of self-made people who wish to enter the service at a later stage cannot avail this opportunity. In effect, the current recruitment process retains its élite bias.

This élite bureaucracy with its guaranteed job for life, (unless one gets in the bad books of the political masters), skillfully cultivates its relationship with self-serving politicians, business and powerful in the society. In the process, they significantly contribute in the development of what Bardhan called a coalition of well-off farmers, industrialists and business, who use resources to feather their own nests rather than building the productive capacity of the Indian economy (Varshney 1984)

While the colonial power was well served by this model, which to a large extent was responsible for fostering poverty and oppression in the colonial days, it has failed to serve a developing economy like India's adequately. Without fundamentally changing the structure and essential nature of the inherited institutions—the most important of which is administrative apparatus and the bureaucracy—development focussed administration will remain ineffective and the inherited bureaucracy will not only continue to operate as previously, but will flourish with the new opportunities available to further its group interests. A closed economy, power to dispense favour in the form of licenses and permits, comparatively poor salary conditions, political ineptitude of governments, and service conditions which are more suitable for a feudal society have all contributed in the performance of the Indian bureaucracy over the last five decades.

Recently a study of Indian Administrative Service (IAS) officers found that many of them do not value the leadership qualities of creativity, institution building, team building and motivation. Furthermore, a most disturbing factor is that among the direct recruits (the 'cream' of the service) there is a greater tendency to indulge in power games, manipulate patronage for personal benefit and shy away from public scrutiny and accountability, while the promoted officers assign higher value to those qualities (Bhattacharya 1997). Promoted officers constitute only a small proportion of the higher echelons of the bureaucracy.

Even in societies which have much more regard for the rule of law and the supremacy of the Parliament have often had difficulty directing the bureaucracy not to be self-serving and to strictly follow government policies. A well respected Australian Minister in the Hawke Government in the 1980s expressed this view when the Minister found that a few senior members of the bureaucracy were stifling his efforts to genuinely focus on community issues, and not just market led financial issues in providing community services to the underprivileged areas in metropolitan centres of Australia.[45] It is not surprising that many consider the popular British comedies *Yes Minister* and *Yes Prime Minister* as good documentaries, not comedies.

The bureaucracy's record over the last 50 years is in many ways less than satisfactory. It not only failed to meet the challenges of a development administration, but also to effectively administer established policies. This is spectacularly reflected in the growth of a black economy in the country. By failing to administer country's tax laws properly the bureaucracy enabled a section of the community to amass a large amount of ill gotten money.

To unearth black money the Government declared amnesty for tax evaders four times since 1965, asking them to declare their income to tax authorities with no questions asked concerning how they procured their undeclared income. Each time amnesty was declared threat of punitive action at the end of the amnesty period was highly publicised (Bhargava 1997). Two questions are relevant. First, if bureaucracy was doing its job properly how could this situation develop in the first place? Second, even if it is assumed that for some unexplainable reasons many cases of tax avoidance initially could not be detected, why was the threat of punitive action not pursued after the first amnesty? No other evidence is required to demonstrate that the bureaucracy, in one of the most crucial areas of government machinery, failed in discharging its responsibilities as required under the principles of good governance policy.

The bureaucracy's failure to perform its duties, and to show its commitments to serve the people can be found at the central as well as at state levels. They further their own interest by playing into the

45 At a private discussion with the author, who was a staff member in the Minister's department.

hands of politicians so much so that the Patna High Court recommended that Bihar was a fit case for President's rule in 1997 under Article 356 of the Constitution. This judgement was given by a Division Bench while adjudicating on a public interest litigation petition that the state bureaucracy was siding with the corrupt people, namely the politicians who were accused of misappropriation of funds.[46]

V The Judiciary's Role

The Indian judiciary has shown unprecedented initiative during the last few years. Amongst other things, it did not hesitate to direct the executive to pursue a certain line of action while hearing public interest applications. In spite of huge public support for such decisions, the dangers of such judicial activism should not be underestimated. In this context, the words of a former Supreme Court justice are worth noting: the independence of the judiciary is a myth as the political environment influences the court's decisions (Roy 1997).

The recent judicial activism has virtually been forced upon it by the weight of circumstances—when the executive is flouting almost all good governance principles, particularly in terms of investigating corruption at the highest levels. The judiciary, on the strength of a large number of public interest applications made to it on behalf of concerned citizens, was forced to assume a specific executive role in the interests of justice. However, the judiciary itself is justifiably concerned with such a large number of public interest applications. A number of jurists and political commentators have already expressed their concern that such practices can not cure the decadence of the constitutional process. Even the Chief Justice of the Supreme Court cautioned the legal community against misuse of public interest litigation and emphasised the need for its proper regulation.[47]

Overall, there have been lapses in the judicial system as well. A High Court Chief Justice was on the verge of being impeached by the

---

46 The *Statesman Weekly*, 1997. 'Bihar fit case for Central Rule', Calcutta, 13 August.

47 Verma, Mr Justice J.S., 1997, in his key note address at a function organised by the Supreme Court Bar Association to commemorate 48th Law Day (26 November) in New Delhi, the day on which the Constitution was born and adopted.

Parliament but avoided it by resigning his position; another was forced to resign for indiscretion, and judges have been found to be corrupt as well. The Executive has manipulated the appointment of judges (the appointment of a Chief Justice during Mrs Gandhi's emergency rule violating established practice is an example), and a few of the judges are not perceived to be honest and impartial in their judicial role.

An Indian jurist observed in 1989 that 'Decline in the Supreme Court's relevance has kept pace with the decline in its prestige' (Noorani 1989b). Even if it is assumed that the Indian courts did not make any unreasoned decisions (depending upon whose viewpoint one accepts), the age-old saying *justice delayed is justice denied* is well and truly evident in the institutional failures in India. It is estimated that there were about 25 million cases pending in courts all over the country in 1996 (Ray 1998). In such circumstances only rich or wealthy institutions can expect the judicial system to benefit them, as the majority of the population will not have the resources to pursue justice for a lengthy period.

Money and political connections have often been used by the wealthy and powerful in society to subvert the judicial process. One of many such cases is the recent Ashok Jain case—it is alleged he violated India's foreign-exchange regulations. By skillfully manipulating the legal system and allegedly using political connections innumerable hurdles were created for the investigating agency (Irani 1998). Even though most of the judges are upright and remain committed to the oath they made, the legal system itself often makes judges helpless, as can be seen from rulings in a number of important cases in recent years.

Notwithstanding their lapses, one must acknowledge that courts are playing an important role in raising public awareness on good governance practices and civil society issues. However, this is limited to the educated urban class who place high value on these issues. The great rural majority would hardly have felt any impact of the courts' active role in this area.

While in recent years the Indian judiciary has shown unprecedented concern for clean administration, at the end of the day it often found that either its instructions were not fully adhered to, or that the prosecuting agency manipulated the investigation and evidence in a way which left no alternative but for the court to dismiss the charges, although it was obvious that had the prosecution followed the investigation properly many cases would not have ended in acquittal. There are many such examples.

For example, it was alleged that Congress received contributions to the tune of nearly 38 million Indian rupees from overseas companies in violation of the Foreign Contribution Regulation Act (FCRA), which bans receipt of donations by political parties from foreign countries and stipulates stringent punishment. The matter was before the Delhi High Court when the Government of India advised the High Court that it had closed the case and that no further investigation into the case by any agency anywhere would be carried out. On receiving this submission, the Division Bench of the High Court observed 'It was for the court to reach any conclusion and the decision whether there was any further scope to an inquiry should also be left to the court as the matter was before it.'[48] The Court's concern about the Government's action was further highlighted when it later issued another order and asked the Central Government to place on record the share holding pattern of the four companies which allegedly donated the funds.[49]

Another interesting case relates to a very senior political figure against whom a public interest litigation was filed by a citizen stating that the person has amassed wealth disproportionate to his known source of income. The government's investigating agency, the Central Bureau of Investigation (CBI) in its submission to the Court gave a clean chit to the accused but the Court found that the basis for this could not be believed. The Court asked the investigating agency to update this probe by examining the sources of the wealth of the accused's son.[50]

In spite of judiciary's active role in promoting good governance practices, its role cannot be unlimited. First, the judiciary is a reactive not pro-active institution and second, in spite of the fact that it often establishes legal precedence through its interpretation, in general, it deals with past, not future events (Seidman and Seidman 1994:128–9). Furthermore, as the judiciary neither controls the purse nor possesses executive power, its effectiveness depends upon the executive and legislature for the resources to perform its tasks properly and their

---

48 The *Hindusthan Times*, 1997. 'HC flays Govt. for closing case', New Delhi, 28 November.

49 The *Hindusthan Times*, 1997. 'HC seeks FCRA probe details against Congress', New Delhi, 13 December.

50 *The Statesman*, 1997. 'Probe Kesri's son, says HC', and 'Kesri's monthly income Rs1,450', Calcutta, 5 and 18 August.

willingness to execute the court's decisions promptly and appropriately. Many countries where strong public opinion does not back the independence and legal supremacy of the judiciary, its verdicts often remain unimplemented. Alexander Hamilton writing in 1788 foresaw this problem when he noted that of the three arms of the government, judiciary was the weakest. Parliament controls the purse strings, executive holds the sword, the judiciary only passes judgement. It has to rely on the executive to implement its decisions and can only function with the respect of the community' (Cooke 1961:522–3).

VI Corruption: A Major Issue in India

Corruption in the public arena is not a new phenomenon, nor unique to India. It existed in ancient times, the middle-ages and throughout history. Realistically speaking no country is free of corruption. The causes and types of corruption differ (Kilgaard 1997). It became widespread during and after the second World War. The widespread corruption that now exists in many parts of the world is significantly a post-war phenomena, largely created by economic and political opportunities.

While corruption at all levels is abhorrent, earlier many economists and policy makers did not make any explicit assessment that it could adversely affect economic growth and development. The Japanese, South Korean or the Indonesian experience made many believe that high economic growth and development can be achieved in spite of high levels of corruption. The World Bank however predicted that 'Countries that have so far achieved high rates of economic growth despite serious corruption may find themselves paying a high price in the future' (World Bank 1997a:103). Regrettably it did not take any strong measures against corrupt practices in countries where it had the capacity to interfere. The recent economic crises in Asia (particularly South Korea, Thailand and Indonesia) confirms the Bank's prediction. Financial shockwaves created by recent bankruptcies of a few well established Japanese financial institutions also confirm that in the long-run corrupt practices have the capacity to drag down the national, regional and global economy.

Huge development expenditure made by many newly independent and war devastated states, expansion of world trade, existence of the Cold War until recently, lack of accountability and above all lack of political morality provided indirect fillip to the growth of corrupt practices in many countries, both developing and developed, in the second half of this century. Many developed countries until recently not only tolerated corrupt practices in developing countries, they also harboured corrupt leaders to stay in power as it suited their political objectives. There are many such examples in Asia, Africa and Latin America. However, the end of the Cold War has created a better opportunity for developed countries to address this issue effectively.

As a consequence, combating corruption has become a major issue for developed and developing countries, and multilateral agencies during the last decade. The United Nations, World Bank, other multilateral and regional organisations and donor countries all now insist through various mechanism available to them that corrupt practices must be tackled head-on. In addition, non-government agencies such as the Berlin based Transparency International has also been instrumental in focussing on the corruption issue and generating people's concern at grass root levels through its annual survey of business corruption in various countries.

The United Nations initiative in this regard began in 1989 when, with the assistance of the Government of Netherlands, it organised an international seminar on corruption in government which was largely attended by high level officials from developing countries (UN 1990). Since that seminar a number of regional seminars in Asia, Africa and the Americas were held to discuss the corruption issue and how to combat it. The United Nations General Assembly also adopted a number of specific resolutions focussing on international cooperation for crime prevention and criminal justice in the development context, a program of action and so on. In addition, the Organisation for Economic Cooperation and Development (OECD), Council of Europe, the European Union (EU), Organisation of American States (OAS) and some individual African states brought this issue to the forefront along with good governance issues (UN 1995). As a result of these collective efforts, community awareness of corruption in government and business has significantly increased in recent years.

Corruption has been defined in many ways. The dictionary's definition of corruption is simple: dishonesty and illegal behaviour by people in positions of authority or power. The World Bank defines corruption as the abuse of public power for private gain (World Bank 1997a:102). For practical and policy purposes the definition adopted by the 19th

Conference of European Ministers of Justice in Malta in 1994 appears to be more focussed

> '...bribery and any other behaviour in relation to persons entrusted with responsibilities in the public or private sector which violates their duties that follow from their status as a public official, private employee, independent agent or other relationship of that kind and is aimed at obtaining undue advantages of any kind for themselves or others' (UN 1990).

In other words, accountability and abuse of power are key issues in any discourse on corruption matters.

This definition however does not cover political practices which have the potential to encourage corruption. This type of corruption may not be in the form of obtaining personal pecuniary advantage, but nevertheless may lead to offering opportunities to individuals not based on merit, or influencing operational practices or decisions of a political nature to suit a particular brand of ideology or perpetuate any particular order or system. The existence of these types of practices is well known and documented, particularly in totalitarian states where political dissidents were often denied many opportunities and or facilities provided by the state to its citizens, without any transparent grounds. Some administrative practices also have the potential to facilitate corrupt practice, although usually they are justified on the grounds that they are part of the Westminster System of government. A former Australian Prime Minister recently raised an interesting point by questioning the Prime Minister's prerogative under the Westminster system to call an election when it suits the ruling party best. He implied that by doing so, the ground becomes uneven and the incumbent may enjoy undue advantage.[51] The American practice of a fixed date for elections which is now a practice in some Australian states and territories does not provide any such scope.

Corruption of heads of state or government, ministers and senior officials on the one hand and the corrupt practices of junior officials on the other have different significance, although they all violate good governance principles. This distinction is highlighted because measures required to fight corruption at different levels have to be different. Corruption at the highest or higher levels is damaging to the fabric of

51 Whitlam, E.G., 1997. Prime Minister on Prime Minister Canberra, A former Australian Prime Minister in a lecture 3 December (unpublished).

the society and has potential to create economic, social and security damages of unprecedented dimension. Because of their positions they also tend to be more sophisticated and posses the resources to prevent, mislead or cover up any investigation; or they can manipulate the system to their advantage by using their political power. Direct financial costs of bribes paid to politicians and senior civil servants are escalating. The United Nations estimates that some heads of states can be bribed for about US$5 million (UN 1995).

Corruption by clerks or petty officers, although equally detested and condemnable, may not be so hard to clamp down on, as they do not have the same string pulling power to manipulate their cases in the event they are prosecuted or found guilty on corruption charges.

Questions therefore need to be asked why corrupt practices develop and how they can flourish for so long as is the case in India now? There are many circumstances under which corruption can grow and flourish. Some of the major reasons are

- excessive controls and regulations encouraging regulators in cohort with politicians to seek rent as people in such an environment always want decisions to favour them
- disappearance of transparency in the decision making process
- accountability is ignored to suit personal and sectional interests in violation of established rules and practices; and failure to properly supervise the decisions and actions of subordinate staff either because they are ineffective or because superiors themselves are involved in reaping benefits of corrupt practices
- limited opportunities for government officials for vertical movement
- perpetrators of corrupt practices when identified remain unpunished
- the non-existence of role models with whom the community can identify.

Normally corruption flourishes under following circumstances

- lack of institutionalised mechanisms to address corrupt practices
- even when such mechanisms existed, operators of the system found it more convenient for one reason or another not to follow the system

- when the established mechanism is not followed, accountability suffers
- with the gradual erosion of accountability, a coalition of bureaucrats, politicians and business use the opportunity to further their own group or individual interest, and in the process develop the attitude that they can do anything they like.

Although corruption in India has been going on for some time, four factors have made the situation critical. First, it now pervades the highest echelons of the society at an unprecedented scale. They evade retribution by influencing the administration and the law enforcement agencies to ensure that their power base remains unscathed, and they do not have to suffe· the harsh realities of daily life in remand centres or behind bars. Second, corruption is no longer considered by many to be morally unacceptable or shameful. Third, lack of an appropriate institutional set-up which could effectively challenge corrupt practitioners at the highest level; and finally the lack of political leadership committed to fight corruption.

There are many such examples when people in high positions have used their connections or have manipulated the administration to their own advantage and benefit. Recently, when the Patna High Court ordered the arrest of a former chief minister on corruption charges, the state jail manual was not observed. Normally, visitors are required to obtain permission to see remand prisoners. In this case this clause was waived for all important persons who wanted to see the prisoner.[52] The question remains what are the criterion used to determine who is an important person? This is important because the accused organised his wife to replace him as chief minister even though she was not a member of the legislature. However, the constitution allows this provided the person gets elected in the legislature within six months of taking office. In this particular case, the new chief minister had never been known to be active in the political arena, exposed to any direct or indirect political situations or previously occupied any public office. These factors strengthen the claims of political opponents that this arrangement will ensure that the accused person, through his wife, would continue to control the administration. The accused was also given the comfort to be remanded in a government guest house converted to a remand centre with all the facilities for comfortable

52 Verma, N., 1997. 'VIPs need no permit to visit former Bihar CM', *The Statesman*, Calcutta, 18 August.

living.[53] It is worth noting that such facilities are not available to ordinary remand prisoners.

Notwithstanding recent spurts in widespread corruption, corrupt practices at the highest level in India have been tolerated for some time. Although many at the highest level may not be individually corrupt in the past, they from time to time through their actions harboured corrupt practices, and in certain cases assisted their political supporters in covering up corrupt practices (Noorani 1973). The effect of these actions can be profound not only amongst their followers, but also on ordinary members of the society. They signal that the right political connections may assist in avoiding retribution. In hindsight one would not be too wrong in concluding that they are perhaps a precursor to the extensive corruption at the highest levels of Indian society.

Amongst many such instances, three cases are highlighted here to demonstrate the impact of the leaderships' behaviour in the development of corrupt practices over the years. First, in 1945 the veteran freedom fighter Prakasham was presented with large sums of money by ordinary citizens which he kept for personal use. People were outraged at this as the funds were presented to assist the independence movement and not Prakasham personally. At this a three member committee was appointed (Messrs Nehru, Patel and Rajendra Prasad) by the Congress party to examine this case. The committee exonerated Prakasham from any wrong doing. People were not satisfied at this and their rage did not subside either. Eventually Mahatma Gandhi stepped in and by exerting his moral authority forced Prakasham to return the entire amount to the party fund.

The second case relates to a senior cabinet member who was alleged to have assisted a businessman in avoiding tax and customs duty. When the issue became public and there were strong calls for public inquiry the Prime Minister resisted the call. Following huge public pressure the Prime Minister appointed his Attorney General to investigate the charges. The Attorney General exonerated the minister on four out of the six charges raised. By initially resisting the call for an inquiry, the wrong signal was again given to the community.

The third such case related to the Prime Minister supporting a cabinet colleague who was forced to resign following the findings of an

53 Yadav, J.P., 1997. 'Laloo sent to air conditioned jail', *The Asian Age*, Calcutta, 31 July.

independent inquiry by a High Court judge. The Minister concerned was not blameless in that corruption case. The Prime Minister wrote to his departing colleague that despite the finding of the Commission, so far as he was concerned, the minister's part in the matter was small, and that the minister even did not know what was done. The Chairman of the Commission was universally respected for his impeccable honesty and judicial integrity. Again conveying the wrong message to the community.

These examples highlight the importance of those who are in power and considered to be the leaders of the nation providing the right signals to the community.

Major corruption cases in India during the last two decades involve people in high positions. Almost all alleged perpetrators have remained unpunished or the cases have remained unresolved. The community remains convinced that inadequate investigation, weak prosecution, and political manipulation and interference at all levels are responsible for alleged offenders escaping retribution. Indeed, none of these cases may stand the scrutiny of an open court, but the community must feel that everything possible has been done to bring the perpetrators to justice, and that the investigating agencies' work was not tampered with. A short summary of recent major corruption cases allegedly involving politicians, bureaucrats, and businesses is provided in Appendix One.

Even before these high profile corruption cases surfaced, a number of researchers and investigators found that corrupt practices became entrenched in the Indian administrative and political system during the last four decades. A 1984 study to determine on what basis transfer of officials takes place in the Irrigation Department in a South Indian state found that fixed rate payments were required to get posted to some work stations. Rates of payment to influence posting decisions vary depending upon the level of position. The study found that both local and higher level politicians were beneficiaries of this arrangement. The researcher recorded an interview where a chief engineer's assistant on personal administration matters (transferring authority) allegedly said 'Frankly we are subjected to a lot of pressures from politicians. Politicians are scum of their country, they are dragging it down.' The study also found that any department which had the power to inflict costly fines or inflict financial loss by their action could raise money, and therefore commanded a price for posting in certain high income areas. For example, the Labour Department by not enforcing legislation, and the Forestry department or departments allocating licenses or subsidies can raise money by using their powers to enforce laws and regulations. Compared to these departments, payments for transfers were totally unknown in the Department of Archives (Wade 1984).

A study of the Koshi river project (in Bihar) in the late 1970s found that contractors were obliged to pay about 40 per cent of the billed amount to supervisory and office staff to receive payments for the work performed by them (Pant 1979). An English national daily in 1982 also reported that in Bihar Rs50,000 was required to be paid for a transfer to a lucrative post. This money, it was alleged, found its way to the minister concerned to the Chief Minister.[54] Nobody would assume that a report in a newspaper is necessarily authentic. However, given the existence of widespread popular perception, and given the poor administration record of many states, the report is more likely to be true than false.

Government's own Santhanam Committee on the prevention of corruption in 1960s also found similar evidence. Nearly 30 years have passed since the Santhanam Committee report and these studies, but situation has not changed. If anything, it has deteriorated and prices have soared, keeping pace with inflation.

Again, it would be wrong to assume that the problem is limited to only a few poorly administered states. Even in the states which are believed to be better administered, these practices are alleged to be well established. A university teacher in an eastern state recently in an interview vouched to the author that even the selection for a position in an academic institution (which is now centrally conducted) would not guarantee the job unless money is exchanged at the clerical level, lest the file go missing and not reappear before the selection lapses. A private bus owner who operates in a metropolitan region confessed during an interview that he was obliged to pay Rs 500 a month to each of the four police stations through which the bus operates. Non-payment of such rent money would ensure that on one pretext or other bus would be forced off the road, denying the owner an income from his investment. It is no wonder that the safety record of bus operators is very poor and the structural safety of many of such buses remain questionable.

---

54 Bhattacharjee, A., 1982. 'In benighted Bihar', *Indian Express*, New Delhi, 2 January.

From the President and the Prime Minister down, the government has used every available opportunity to invite the community to fight the evils of corruption. Yet some of the actions (or inaction) of the government clearly indicate that people in high positions are actively working to protect highly placed people accused in corruption cases. For example, the Prime Minister removed the CBI Director (Singh) on 30 June 1997 when he was overseas on the grounds that he was not happy with the officer's performance. Nobody could question the Prime Minister's authority to do so for the reason given in his transfer order. However, investigative journalists claim that the real reason was somewhat different. The issue is if the reason for transfer given by the Government is valid than how could the discharged officer be promoted to a higher level position as Special Secretary, Ministry of Home Affairs?

Two issues require clarification. First, if the officer was found to be ineffective in a junior position, on what basis was he promoted and transferred to a senior position in the Department of Home Affairs. No wonder, long before Singh was unceremoniously transferred from his position, a headline in a respected national daily with tongue in cheek wrote 'Joginder Singh was doing something right!'[55] Second, by violating every established practice why was a superannuated officer who was already on extension appointed to replace the deposed officer at a time when the agency was investigating a number of criminal cases involving highly placed politicians and bureaucrats? The newly appointed officer by assuming office directed that only on exceptional circumstances accused politicians or civil servants would be arrested.[56] This direction implies that the investigating agency was unlikely to take decisions based on the outcome of investigation of individual cases. Would it therefore not be unreasonable to conclude that a superannuated officer was more likely to follow the unwritten dictates of his political masters in pursuing corruption cases?

The arbitrary transfer of officials has been a major factor in the development of a politician-bureaucratic nexus in corruption. Government from time to time has used its power to transfer officials to punish independent minded officers when it felt threatened that the officer was too upright and could not be cajoled to meet unlawful

55 The *Statesman Weekly,* 1997. Calcutta, 24 May.

56 *Bartaman* (Metropolitan daily), 1997. 'No more indiscriminate arrest: Sharma', Calcutta, 1 July.

wishes of the executive (Noorani 1987). The Director of the National Academy of Administration has voiced his concerns in a paper on demoralisation in the Indian Administrative Service on account of the scourge of indiscriminate transfers and victimisation of morally upright officers by their superiors. The report of the Vohra committee has brought into the open the unholy nexus of politician-criminal-police bureaucrat-judge (Bhattacharya 1997b). This position is frankly admitted by the service people themselves in a recent study (Singh and Bhandarker 1997). And yet, unsatisfactory institutional arrangements are still maintained allowing many alleged corruption cases to not be addressed to the satisfaction of the general public or the informed sections of the community who are keen to stamp out corruption from public life.

In addition to the arbitrary power to transfer, the practice of dismissing public servants without assigning a transparent reason also has significant potential to lead to corruption. The potential threat of dismissal without assigning any transparent reason may be a sufficient reason for some public servants to play it safe by providing advice sweet to the ears of their political masters, irrespective of their appropriateness, thus perpetuating policy corruption. This becomes particularly important when it involves senior level public servants, one of whose two principal responsibilities is to provide independent advice on policy issues to the government of the day. For example, political and newspaper commentators have not discounted this possibility when eight departmental secretaries, both permanent and contracted, were sacked during 1996–97 in Australia before their term expired without assigning any reason following the election of a new government at the federal level.[57] Nobody would question a government's right to sack officials on transparent and legitimate grounds, but to do so without assigning reason is pregnant with corruption possibilities. The United States' practice of appointing contributors to campaign funds or people who are close to the seat of power to senior government positions is also a type of corruption. It is a matter of conjecture whether this practice has adversely impacted on the US policy development process; opinions vary.

In India the situation has deteriorated to such an extent that the judiciary now occasionally plays the role of *de facto* executive. The

57 The *Canberra Times,* 1998. 'Howard disposes his generals', editorial, Canberra, 5 January.

Patna High Court, on receipt of an contempt application that a senior investigating officer in charge of a major corruption case against a powerful politician be transferred out of the investigation because he was not prepared to compromise the investigation, ordered on 4 August 1997 that the officer could not be removed by the executive without prior agreement of the Court and the Court would ensure that its order was carried out by the administration.[58]

Although corruption and criminal activities are considered synonymous, there exist subtle but very important distinction between these two. Economic and policy corruption distorts the functioning of the economy, but when money controls the political machine or influences government policies and activities, it threatens the existence of a civil society.

As mentioned earlier, involvement of politicians and senior bureaucrats in criminal activities is not new or unique to India alone. However, what is new is that other countries are making every effort to address this issue constructively, whereas India only pays lip service to the eradication or reduction of corrupt practices. The Vohra (a former Home Secretary) Committee report on the criminalisation of politics unequivocally stated that the Mafia, with the blessing of politicians, was virtually running a parallel government in India. These forces have become so powerful that they even dare to influence the highest judicial official. The Chief Justice of India publicly stated at the Court that he and his colleagues on the Jain Hawla case had come under persistent pressure to withdraw. He further revealed

> All types of things began happening to me and the same things are happening to my brother judges. We are getting all types of calls with some persons trying to reach us and influence us.[59]

Eradication of corruption is not easy. It is a social issue as much as a law enforcement issue. Governments often make the mistake of taking actions without due consideration of all relevant factors. As a result measures fail to achieve their objectives, and in the process the peoples' faith in the governments' capacity to fight corruption

---

58 A Patna High Court Division Bench judgement on two contempt petitions brought against top state officials in connection with the Animal Husbandry corruption case; Patna, 4 August 1997.

59 Verma, Mr Justice J.S., 1997. 'I am under too much pressure on Hawla', Chief Justice of India, New Delhi, in a statement at the Court on 14 July before proceedings in the case commenced.

diminishes. Second, in many developing countries there exists a tendency to follow blindly what has been practiced in overseas countries. Corruption and criminal practices although often influenced by overseas conditions, primarily reflect an individual society's values, perceptions and their national and community objectives. It is therefore important that countries wishing to establish mechanisms to fight corruption and criminal activities at the highest levels of society should carefully examine all options available to them and then develop a comprehensive strategy to fit their own situation.

A number of countries in recent years have achieved success in addressing corruption issues—amongst them are Uganda, Tanzania and Hong Kong. The Peoples' Republic of China has also recently taken steps to stem corrupt practices, but it has been much less successful in achieving its objective compared to the other countries mentioned above. Among developed countries two Australian states (Queensland and New south Wales) have addressed police, bureaucratic and political corruption issues comprehensively. While it is for India to decide which organisational form it should adopt to address its own situation, the experience of these countries would assist in developing an appropriate strategy to fight both corruption and criminalisation of the political system.

Uganda has concentrated on cleaning up the civil service (World Bank 1997a:106). It recognises that it will take long time. Some of the important measures adopted are

- policy reform and deregulation to remove opportunities for rent seeking
- civil service reform to streamline the public work force
- improved remuneration
- providing training and instilling a code of ethics at all levels involving public officials; and
- prosecution of corruption.

It has established an Office of the Inspector General of Government in 1988 to investigate, among other things, corruption on a permanent basis. The office is charged with the duty of eliminating corruption and abuse of public office, and the detection and prevention of corruption in public office. Other measures introduced are activating and strengthening the Public Accounts Committee (a standing Committee of Parliament) and the Auditor General's office; development of a leadership code; improving accountability and transparency within public administration and by making government business open to public control. Most importantly, the Inspector General does not report to the chief executive officer, but to the legislature (Ruzindana 1995:191–208).

Tanzania has established an Office of Prevention of Corruption Bureau within the President's Office which has addressed the issue from a number of angles. It is, by various means, encouraging political parties to address and fight corruption practices by effective use of law, by ensuring that they are enforced without discrimination and by actively promoting social engineering policies to expose and fight corrupt practices. The office insists that

> if there has to be success the [anti-corruption] campaign must involve all and sundry—the public and private sectors...At the same time the public servants must not only appear transparent but must be seen to be so (Muganda 1985:481–98).

Tanzania's efforts received international recognition and praise from many quarters because of the commitment of its political leadership. President Mkapa on his election made full disclosure of his assets and those of his spouse. He instituted the Wariobs Commission, a distinguished jurist of the highest integrity who promptly produced a report the likes of which few countries have ever seen. It lambasted the country's institutions and their leaders, without exception, for the perilous state the country was in. In spite of the political sensitivity of the report, the President immediately released it to the press, inviting a barrage of criticism. He publicly challenging his Ministers to put their respective houses in order in spite of the fact that he was walking on an electoral tight-rope.[60]

Hong Kong was riddled with corruption in the 1960s, particularly in its police force. In 1974 the Governor General established the Independent Commission Against Corruption (ICAC) primarily focussing on police corruption. The Commission is independent of the police force and reports directly to the Governor. It has the power to investigate and prosecute corruption cases as well as to sponsor a public education campaign. During its existence it has faced number of difficulties. The success of the Commission to a significant extent is attributed to government's appointment of a person of unquestioned integrity as the

---

60 Transparency International, 1997. *Annual Report*, Berlin.

first head of the commission, and to a policy of investigating and prosecuting 'big tigers' from the outset (World Bank 1997a:107). In spite of many obstacles and difficulties it had achieved considerable success in fighting corruption. Public surveys carried out between 1977 and 1994 indicate that public perception of corruption has fallen significantly. Indirect evidence also suggests that active corruption has declined as well.

In terms of social complexity none of the above countries are comparable to India. China on the other hand is a large and complex country like India. China's political corruption is caused by

- traditional norms and values—instrumental use of lasting personal connections, the overriding loyalty owed to kinsmen and primary groups
- economic conditions—poverty, scarcity, bottlenecks and supply problems
- structural factors—lack of structural restraints, the role of state markets
- changing élite composition—the Communist party consisted mostly of guerrilla-type cadres of peasant background, but since then become the only available career structure for attaining social mobility and power
- and finally, following the revolution individual experienced a pace of social change so fast that the older, traditional norms being eradicated were not being replaced in time.

The Chinese government has adopted a number of measures to address the corruption issue focussing on education, establishing Discipline Inspection Commissions (DICs) at all levels and administrative reform by simplifying procedures and rules (Ostergaard 1986). China's concern is clear from the large number of steps it has taken to stamp out corruption. For example, it has established corruption reporting centres, telephone hot lines and publicises reports of punishments meted out to state and party cadres for misconduct. However the question remains whether such anti-corruption measures can be enforced, when corruption by many accounts has become the norm (Conner 1989:8–14). It is clear that in spite of the differences in government and political structures in China some of the causes of corruption there are similar to India. While China's methods may not be suitable for India, they at least would provide some insight to the effectiveness of various anti-corruption methods applied in a society as complex as India's.

The anti-corruption measures adopted by the New South Wales and Queensland state governments in Australia are comprehensive and have been successful to a large extent in fighting or at least in challenging the police, business and political corruption. They have established independent agencies and appear to be operating effectively. Both these agencies are independent of the executive, although in Queensland the agency is in severe disagreement with the executive.

In Queensland the Criminal Justice Commission (CJC) was established in 1989 after an extensive investigation by an independent commission of inquiry, following media revelations, on crime and corruption in the state. The CJC is permanently charged with the monitoring, reviewing, coordinating and initiating reform of the administration of criminal justice including those criminal justice functions not appropriately carried out by the police or other agencies (CJC 1990).

Its mandate is extensive which includes enhancing awareness of the problems at various levels, exposing corruption and misconduct in all units of public administration, collating and providing evidence for prosecution. The agency is independent of the executive. It reports to the Parliament directly although it liaise with a Parliamentary Select Committee (known as Parliamentary Criminal Justice Committee)to appraise it on CJC's functions, focus etc. The agency has achieved significant success in attacking corrupt practices both at the administrative and political levels. Its success can be attributed to the high-quality selection and independence of its senior officers

In NSW the Independent Commission Against Corruption (ICAC) was established in 1988 at the political initiative of the government of the day with the objective to restore the integrity of public administration and public institutions in the state. In addition to its investigatory responsibilities, its charter also includes to assist in developing sound management practices and making public officials more aware of what it means to hold an office of public trust and more aware of the detrimental effects of corrupt practices. The Commission has significant coercive power to force people to give evidence before it.

Its functions include investigative; policy making—review and revision of methods of work, procedures, laws and practices; advisory; educative and communicating to appropriate authorities, the results of investigations. The success to date is significant and again is due to the leadership provided by the Commission itself. It also reports directly to the Parliament (ICAC 1989).

The experience of these countries can provide important insights for developing an effective strategy to fight corruption and criminal activities at the highest level in India. While developing anti-corruption strategies four things must be kept in mind to ensure success. First, the designated agency responsible for fighting corruption must be fully independent and should only be answerable to the Parliament, and not to the executive. Second, it should be provided with appropriate budgetary and logistic support to carry out its task, because initially it will face opposition from various and unexpected corners of the society as many will feel threatened by the agency's initiatives. Thirdly, every person appointed in this agency should be thoroughly vetted for their integrity and commitment to fight corruption, and all senior persons must have the community's unreserved respect and confidence. The Hong Kong example clearly shows the importance of community's confidence in fighting corruption against many odds and difficulties.

Finally, there should not be any special legal provisions to protect public officials or senior bureaucrats from prosecution, as is the current practice. The agency responsible for fighting corruption should be able to face criticisms if it fails to perform according to its charters and be prepared to pay for its major failures in personal and monetary terms. The agency will be unable to gain the community's respect and trust if it does not operate with the same laws for everybody. The capacity to command the respect and trust of the community is a vital element in the fight against corruption, as shown by the Hong Kong and Tanzanian experience.

In summary, the five mantras of the anti-corruption drive following Klitgaard (1997) are: monopolies must be reduced and carefully regulated; official discretion must be clarified; accountability must be enhanced; the probability of being caught must increase; and penalties for corruption (both givers and takers) must rise. It is a tall order, but there is no short cut when corruption has engulfed society as a whole like an uncontrolled bushfire in summer.

Chapter Four: The Needed Reforms

I International Push for Administrative Reform

Public administration underwent metamorphic changes during the last two decades in many countries, particularly in the Commonwealth (United Kingdom, New Zealand, Australia, Canada, Malaysia, Singapore and Malta). The Commonwealth, United Nations and the World Bank have all been encouraging countries to reform their administrative systems to meet the challenges of coming decades. They all agree that a monolithic bureaucratic structure cannot be considered a repository of all wisdom, and that it may not be appropriate to satisfy the needs of the 21st Century. The collective focus of these countries is directed at

- making the staff, government and management more efficient
- improving quality of services, the management of finance and the policy making; and
- increasing partnership with organisations and agencies outside the government.

The Commonwealth focuses on a distillation and analysis of innovations and best practices in public service management across the Commonwealth countries (Wettenhall 1996:517–9). It does not direct member countries on how to reform the public service; on the contrary it encourages innovations in thinking about its role and functioning in a federally structured government; about service users; about administrative structures and about staff. It stresses that managerial pragmatism and political conviction are essential to motivate management innovations in government (Kaul 1997:13–26).

The United Nations General Assembly in 1996 also highlighted the need for administrative reform. While it actively encouraged every member nation to give priority to administrative reform issues, at the same time it emphasised that there should not be a single model for good governance practices and public administration structure; each country should develop a structure to meet its individual requirements (United Nations 1996:513–6). The World Bank also insists that administrative reform is an essential requirement to manage development. It suggests that three parties namely, politicians, the bureaucracy and the community need to be twined to achieve reform in governance and administrative practices (World Bank 1989).

An important lesson from the various reform measures introduced in other countries is that whatever mechanism is adopted, the system must be flexible because governments in a rapidly changing economic and political environment are required to respond in short notice. No country in such circumstances would wish to be constrained by a rigid administrative system limiting its capacity to respond to these changes quickly and effectively. Focus should therefore be on establishing operating procedures that are a mix of rules and standards as well as informal conventions and consultations. Given India's failure during the last 50 years to establish healthy constitutional and administrative conventions, and given that unscrupulous people can use flexible systems corruptly, the reform measures in India need to be carefully conceived, designed and applied.

It is now universally recognised that truly democratic government assists economic development. The study by Professor Sen found that countries which had a democratic form of administration had not suffered famine lends significant credence to the above (Sen 1984). Any administrative and political reform strategy therefore must begin by considering how best to reinforce democratic values, particularly those values which are considered part of a civil society, and encourage an open and accountable government. Opponents of such reform initiatives could argue that India has maintained her democratic form of government against many odds, and hence there is no need for such initiative. In response to such arguments, it must be reaffirmed that to establish a democratic form of government is one thing, but to imbibe democratic principles in government and administration by effectively promoting the values of a civil society is another.

In a democracy commitment to Westminster principles and practices is considered essential. Nevertheless in a rapidly changing world some of these principles and practices need reassessment and require modification to ensure that the true spirit of a democratic form of government can be faithfully maintained. Even in countries such as the United Kingdom where the Westminster principle is firmly rooted, people increasingly feel excluded from public decisions impacting on their lives and are loosing confidence in the political process or in their own representatives (World Bank 1997a:110–11). The growth of rigid party systems has contributed to this alienation and yet, without a stable and organised political party system the management of government business can become chaotic.

Experts in governance issues need to focus their attention on developing a more participatory mechanism which would ensure both a stable government and an effective participation in government by its citizens, if citizens are not to feel disenchanted with the political process. Recently a British Broadcasting Corporation (BBC) Survey in the United Kingdom found that the general public had grown tired and bored with political interviews because the interviewees generally refuse to answer specific questions and stick rigidly to the party line.[61]

Many constitutional purists will no doubt abhor the idea of tinkering with the long established Westminster principles. But consider the following: national economies no longer operate independently; they are intricately linked up with global economy both in an operational and legal sense; signatories of the WTO agreement are obliged to follow its regulations. On wider environmental and human rights issues similar internationalism is taking place. Increasingly nation-governments are committing themselves to abide by internationally accepted norms on issues such as human rights and the control of illicit drug trafficking. Failure to achieve these internationally perceived benchmarks on such issues not only invites international condemnation, but also erring countries are placed under immense pressure through the various avenues available to the international community.

Reform efforts therefore must begin by reassessing Westminster principles within each individual country's historical, social and community nuances. The few economically and socially successful countries in post-colonial Asia and Africa successfully adopted a modified version of Westminster principles as a basis for their government. Malaysia and Mauritius' approach to managing their multi-ethnic societies may not appear to fully conform with traditional Westminster principles, but they clearly show that a slightly modified approach by preserving the core values of a democratic form of government could bring larger benefits to society (World Bank 1997a:113).

61 Australian Broadcasting Corporation, 1998. Political Commentary in its Midday Program, 29 January; also, in the *Canberra Times*, 9 February.

II Constitutional Issues

The Indian constitution and the post-independent administrative system failed to take into full consideration issues such as its past history, social relationships and so on. This has not contributed to the growth of a healthy participatory government and neither has it encouraged good governance principles to take firm root in India.

There are a number of reasons for this outcome.

- A Westminster style of democracy presupposes an informed and literate constituency. Indian adult illiteracy rate even after half a century of independence is about 49 per cent of the population.
- In order for a democracy to succeed an all round loyalty to the democratic process itself is required (Leftwich 1993). In the Indian case, as can be seen from the events that have unfolded to date, this loyalty has been missing.
- The failure of successive governments to contribute in the growth of a truly federal structure in which the diverse nature of India would have found ground to flourish and prosper.
- Conventions play a significant part in interpreting provisions of any written constitution. Regrettably, the Indian political leadership singularly failed to develop a healthy constitutional convention which would have satisfied the focus of the constitutional provisions.

While features of the Indian Constitution are sound, it must be recognised that these were included without really establishing whether they would suit Indian conditions. It is interesting to note that this situation is not unique to India alone. Many countries with a colonial history have found themselves in the same situation, and this was acknowledged long before colonies started gaining independence in the post second world-war period. For example, a similar sentiment was unequivocally expressed by Balfour when he wrote that constitutions were easily copied, temperaments were not, and if it should happen that the borrowed constitution and the temperament fail to correspond, the misfit may have serious results (Balfour 1936).

History is full of examples which confirm that in the absence of a focussed common objective, more mundane concerns and daily needs of communities dominate peoples' attention where self, tribal, ideological or regional interests often dominate. To overcome such a situation and to tell people to focus on one or few overwhelming objectives requires an extraordinary political and leadership skill. One could recall leadership such as Sukorno in Indonesia, Nkruma in Ghana or Gandhi in India whose unquestionable leadership qualities enabled them to free their countries from colonial rulers. However once the euphoria of independence was over, many of them failed to carry the community with them to make their economic development objectives realised. One possible reason for such failures could have been their inability to conceptualise the hard tasks lying ahead following independence, and lack of an understanding of the path required to achieve such objectives. A hint of this can be found in the famous slogan by the late President of Ghana when he pronounced 'Seek ye first the political kingdom, and all else will follow' (Seidman and Seidman 1994:1). Unfortunately, this is far from reality.

In this context the example of the Chinese leadership throws some light on why—while acknowledging their one-party government system—they succeeded, and many others did not, although many of them at the dawn of their independence enjoyed almost evangelical support of the population they were leading. An American Chinese scholar found 'Mao, no doubt, was a Marxist believer but, he formed his radically revolutionary ideology within the Chinese traditional thinking on power, authority, the ruling and the ruled, and the role of law' (Xin Ren 1997:11). In other words, although Mao's political philosophy was imported, he used the long-standing Chinese Confucian values to ensure that people accept them. Many will argue that people did not voluntarily accept them, but were forced to do so by the party dictatorship. While there may be some grain of truth in this, it is undeniable that China has been able to achieve a higher economic growth rate than India during the last 50 years. China's development is spectacular for two reasons. First, compared to India, China was in a primitive stage of economic development when it became independent in 1949; second, after its fall-out with the former Soviet Union in the 1950s it virtually had to rely on its own resources while India was still receiving significant financial and technological assistance from overseas. This point is raised to emphasise that economic growth and development cannot be seen in isolation from social and political realities. Until recently economists did not give this the attention it deserves, although scholars like Cohen alluded to it more than a quarter of a century ago (Cohen 1974).

During the colonial period the burning desire was to gain independence. In post-independence days people's primary focus was on achieving economic development and an improved standard of living for the population at large. Fifty years have passed but this objective has mostly remained unfulfilled, and the visible benefits of development activities have only been enjoyed by at most a quarter of the population, as the income distribution pattern shows. A 1992 survey found that 20 per cent of the population enjoyed 43 per cent of the income or consumption (World Bank 1997d:55–7). At the same time people—even though they may be illiterate—are increasingly becoming aware of the developments that are taking place in other parts of the world, including places which have somewhat similar historical and societal similarities with India. The advent of improved communication systems, and television in particular has expedited this information dissemination process. In this environment people are asking what makes their position so different from that of people in other places. This urge to question is the most important element in seeking changes to any system when it fails to deliver what was expected of it.

If peoples' reasonable expectations of a higher standard of living cannot be met, their aspirations and enthusiasm cannot be constructively managed by the leadership, these then find expression in unsavoury and unlawful activities. The proliferation of violence on minor pretext is an example. Similar situations can be observed in many other newly independent developing countries.

Although in India's case the Constitution was, in a large part borrowed, it would appear that a few of the framers of the Constitution personally did not believe in some of its important policy aspects. For example, constitutional provisions confirm India's federal structure, but there is evidence that Nehru, India's first Prime Minister, was not committed to the principles of federalism as they are normally understood. Bernard, in a recent paper on how Bengal and Punjab became touch stones and then powder kegs in the nationalist aspirations of both sides in pre-independence days writes

> ...the sulking Punjab and a frustrated Bengal, let us go back to the beginning, i.e. to part II of the Government of India Act (1935), entitled *Federation of India*. Every student of the period knows how Jawharlal Nehru as well as Mohammed Ali Jinnah rejected it outright and in definitive terms (Bernard 1997).

Curiously, Churchill also dismissed it outright.

The success of constitutions and establishment of constitutional morality (which establishes healthy conventions) is closely entwined with the structure of the administration of the country. If the form of administration is not of the same nature as that of the constitution, it is possible to pervert the constitution without changing its form by merely changing the form of administration and making it inconsistent and opposed to the spirit of the constitution (Noorani 1989). The greatest failure of post-independent India lies here as, Brown reconfirms

> India continued to be governed by Nehru in ways which were remarkably similar to those of his imperial predecessors, both in the structure of the state itself, despite the universal adult franchise, and in the style of the administrative services which he had once denounced as anti-national and requiring drastic reform (Brown 1997).

During the last two decades the Indian intelligentsia started pondering on these issues as the country lost its direction towards peace and prosperity. In the 1980s questions were asked whether the Parliamentary system of government suited India, or did it warrant a different system, such as Presidential. Regrettably, while many people were willing to canvass options without necessarily tying them with their party position on this issue, they still failed to address the fundamental issue of how to empower people effectively to exercise their genuine political rights to elect and dismiss governments, and to ensure that people feel part of the government, which they alone can elect. Only when people are genuinely empowered will politicians and political parties feel compelled to follow the peoples' wishes, and not to act to enrich themselves personally. The Centre for Policy Research, recognising this changing mood of the population, commissioned a study to examine the appropriateness of a Presidential system *vis-à-vis* the Parliamentary system (Pai Panadiker 1989), although a wider examination of these issues in their totality is needed.

To understand why in relative terms the Indian socioeconomic situation has deteriorated one also needs to examine who benefited most from the economic policies and the administrative structure during the last fifty years. It is undeniable that India has achieved success in a number of areas. However, the visible benefits of this success have gone to a relatively small portion of the population, which in turn has resulted in a few people—both in rural and urban areas—wielding disproportionate power to influence the policies which benefit them most. This has distorted policy development and implementation. Even when political power was won by the economically or socially poorer sections of the community, they failed to act in a way which could have brought back peoples' confidence in the constitutional and administrative process. Regrettably, the political environment and the administrative system did not provide any established mechanism to ensure that their newly acquired political power was not used to satisfy sectional interests only.

When Laloo Prasad Yadav became Chief Minister of Bihar, he got the opportunity to demonstrate that although Yadavs and other disadvantaged groups suffered in the past under élite upper class rule, his government would ensure that this was not repeated. This hope was short lived as the entire administration was used to advantage his and his group's political interests. He was not doing anything new except that he was following the same route with more vigour than his predecessors. The only difference was that perpetrators of the previous system belonged to a higher socio-economic group as one political commentator wrote 'Some had the class and the style, others did not. But that does not make the former less vulgar than the more obvious, and in a strange kind of way more honest...' (Mustafa 1997).

Similarly, Ms Mayawati on becoming Chief Minister of Uttar Pradesh presented a budget where almost a quarter of the annual plan outlay was earmarked for the welfare schemes for people belonging to her own class (scheduled class and tribes).[62] While no one would object to uplifting the conditions of the underprivileged class, the question is whether the economic and financial situation in the state could justify such huge expenditure for a relatively small section of the community and what would happen to other priority expenditure required for the well being of the state's entire population.

It is evident that on the one hand the spirit of many of the constitutional provisions were not followed during the last fifty years, and on the other hand the administrative structure virtually remained the same as it was pre-independence. Furthermore, the same bureaucracy which followed a ruler and ruled in the colonial days maintained their underlying position by marginally adjusting their *modus operandi* which overall did not benefit the Indian masses. The successive post-independent Indian governments provided only lip service in the name of reforming the administrative structure to serve the new India.

---

62 *The Asian Age*, 1997. 'Mayawati Budget converts UP into Ambedker pradesh', Calcutta, 27 July.

III Administrative Issues

There has been no dearth of studies and investigations on the need to reform the administrative system. There are at least 43 reports available on this subject prepared by various committees and commissions since the days of Lord Curzon in the beginning of this century (Maheswari 1997). The three major studies on public service reform in the post-independent India were the Gorwala Report on Public Administration (1951), Paul Appleby's Survey of Indian Administration (1953) and the Administrative Reforms Commission Report (also known after its Chairman as the Hanumanthaiya Report, 1968). In addition to specific investigations, Parliamentary and Central Pay Commission (one in each decade) reports also made significant recommendations to reform public administration.

Pay commissions recommended pay scales for central government employees along with additional recommendations to reform the service. In most cases a number of inter-connected recommendations were packaged together to make the reform effective, *albeit* by maintaining the existing structure, but in each of these cases government of the day, without exception, adopted the improved pay scales suggested by the respective commissions while most of the reform recommendations fell by the wayside. Most of these recommendations were bypassed either through referring them to a committee of secretaries or other similar bodies which virtually ensured that they would not be pursued vigorously. An interesting point to note is that the secretaries of each of these commissions was a senior bureaucrat, and many believe that bureaucratic involvement in such important positions ensured that the recommendations were couched in a format that did not threaten the power of the Indian bureaucracy.

But more importantly, most of these inquiries failed to grasp the main issues namely: what role the bureaucracy would play in development administration in shaping government's economic policies and what will be bureaucracy's relationship with the government and the people at large, and how will these relationships be administered. Despite these reports, one commentator nicely summed up the situation that

> There has not been any simplification of procedures, no reduction in cross-referencing and consulting various departments, no enforcement of accountability, no structural changes for arresting fissiparous tendencies' (Bhattacharya 1997b).

In summary, past Indian governments of all shades failed to

- articulate the role of civil service in India's development administration
- answer how the bureaucracy will operate in a federal structure? and
- define what relationship the bureaucracy will have with the government, the people and what procedures will be followed to ensure their accountability, integrity and measure their performance.

The following examples highlight some of many such problems. Central civil servants are recruited by the Central Government although their immediate employer is the state government. This arrangement forces them to divide their loyalties between two sets of governments. To make the situation worse, the 72nd and 73rd amendments of the constitution which invested local self government with specific powers will create further confusion on the relationship and the effectiveness of their power at various levels of government.

A vast majority of these reports on India's administrative system only tinkered in peripheral issues, none of them examined the system within the dual context of changed political, economic and social context in the post-independent India on the one hand, and a rapidly changing global economic and political environment on the other. For example, apart from the service delivery responsibility, government and the bureaucracy will be increasingly required to ensure that national policies are not compromised by provisions of the international agreements, protocols and covenants. In addition to a number of United Nations protocols which are not always legally binding, the provisions of the World Trade Organisation are more complex and legally enforceable, and will have a far reaching national economic and political consequences. Many of these protocols will impinge on a gamut of environmental, investment, trade and social policies. These protocols and agreements will significantly influence and impact on domestic policies. This would not have mattered much provided that the countries' economic bases were broadly comparable and similar, and no country was enjoying any economic advantage.

Regrettably, significant differences in countries' economic and social bases exist. Developed industrial countries, particularly the G7 (excluding Russia), although they only have 20 per cent of the world's population wield enormous power through their privileged voting rights in the IMF and the World Bank boards. Over the years it has become clear that when there are conflicts, the will of the economically powerful is forced upon developing countries (Singer 1993). Within this context developing countries' administration need to be extra vigilant and proactive to match the guile and knowledge of their counterparts in developed countries. Failure to do so could result in being out-manoeuvred in far reaching international negotiations (Dasgupta 1997). This would require a bureaucratic and administrative machinery which is knowledgeable, innovative and proactive instead of a file pushing administration keen on maintaining their power base, self-serving and reactive. Although the Indian bureaucracy individually may be capable of addressing these emerging issues, the bureaucracy as an institution has not yet been positioned to perform these tasks effectively and adequately.

These emerging complex policy tasks will require a clear understanding of national issues and priorities, and how these could be fostered within a country's international obligations. To give an example: intellectual property rights and international patent rights under the renegotiated WTO provisions require countries to be aware of the complexities of many such issues and to remain proactive to protect their self interest. The recent success of a United States company in getting a rice grain protected in the name of *Basmati* took the Indian bureaucracy by surprise. Although a lot of noises are now being made, unfortunately India lacked the legal framework to protect plant varieties exclusive to the country, as pointed out by Dr Swaminathan, an internationally well known scientist.[63]

However it cannot be said that this is a sudden development that no body could foresee. Sri Lanka and Kenya have long been engaged in the misappropriation of Indian geographical appellations such as Darjeeling tea. An Indian non-government organisation (Gene campaign) drew the government's attention to India's geographically indicated rights in 1996, but yet no law was in place.[64] This highlights the dimension of policy problems that the bureaucracy and the government would be required to address urgently in the months to come.

There are many other examples which make it clear that the bureaucracy will not be able to perform these tasks on its own. It will

63 The *Economic Times,* 1998, New Delhi, 18 February.
64 The *Economic Times,* 1998, New Delhi, 1 March.

be required to form a coalition with academics, researchers, business and the wider community through non-government organisations to effectively respond to new issues covering uncharted fields. Unless this coalition is carefully structured and appropriately organised, and the relationship mechanism between the coalition partners is clearly defined policy responses to many of these issues will not only be inadequate, but may be dangerously inappropriate and may not serve country's interests either.

Governments in many developed and some developing countries have realised this urgent need to reshape their respective public services to face the economic and social challenges of the 21st Century for some time. While it would be fair to say that all changes implemented and or mooted to date are not necessarily ideal or even may not lead to improvements in the service delivery or policy formulation, nonetheless they are experimenting with new ideas and procedures in service delivery and policy formulation (Ray and May 1996).

IV Reform Priorities For India

Most of the reform issues are interrelated and cannot be considered in isolation. Many of these issues may appear to be innocuous at the outset, but their impact on the development and maintenance of good governance practices are significant. In this connection a fundamental point to remember is that all these issues are intricately interconnected, and each of them influences the performance of the other. The issues are

- constitutional
- parliamentary control over the executive
- public service and public sector reform
- electoral reform, and
- social awareness.

Constitutional

The Indian constitution was adopted by a Constituent Assembly and drafted by a drafting committee. The membership of the Assembly although elected (but not on the basis of universal franchise) was dominated by élites. Drafting committee members were mostly western educated, significantly influenced by western values of legal and constitutional practices, and the Constitution was largely based on the Westminster model (Rustamji 1997). One of the most contentious areas of the Constitution (Article 356), is borrowed almost in its entirety from the Government of India Act of 1935 which was designed by the colonial power for its own benefit and convenience. At that time it was unreservedly condemned by the entire nationalist spectrum (Kaul 1997). Migdal's study of a number of third world countries including India led him to conclude

> ...that Third World societies and states may not fit well into moulds shaped on the basis of European or North American experiences (Migdal 1988:10–41).

If it is accepted that a constitution should reflect the aspirations of its people and realistically reflect their social and economic aspirations, and its capacity to achieve those objectives, then it is doubtful whether the framers of the Indian Constitution truly understood the psyche of the Indian masses, its socioeconomic mosaic and the changing nature of the relationship between pre-colonial, colonial and post-colonial society, and how these changes affected the state-society relationship.

Gandhi was perhaps one of the very few exceptions as he understood the Indian people well, but at that time he had departed the political scene. Prime Minister Nehru, on the other hand, ruled India as undisputed leader during the vital 17 years immediately post-independence. He had, as one historian found, an

> effortless sense of superiority and no experience of hardship or personal challenge...and little knowledge of the India of the vast majority of his compatriots (Brown 1997).

Maulana Azad, a highly respected freedom fighter and leader, a member of the Constituent Assembly and post-independent government acknowledged this failure. A decade later he wrote that there existed wide gulf between leaders and the Indian society (Azad 1960).

Many constitutional rights remain a wish list to most citizens because of deprivation and large scale adult illiteracy. They often fail to see, with some legitimacy, the relevance of good governance principles in their struggle to survive. Under such circumstances, violence and crime are human responses to economic distress and political discontent (Nayar 1975). These are manifested in secessionist movements and the growth of terrorism by one community group against another (for example in the North-East Indian states, Kashmir, Punjab), as is the case in the Balkans. Communal riots or the threat of them are more frequent. In such an environment communities fail to acknowledge even genuine problems and development difficulties facing the country, as their faith has been shattered too many times in the past. This has led to the current feeling of despondency in many parts of the country (Kohli 1992:383–87).

Subramaniam wrote in 1992 that

> The quantity and quality of violence characterising Indian society at all levels today has...[a] political context; in a context of large-scale malfunctioning politics develops an insatiable appetite for all space, both public and private (1992:1).

Another researcher observed a similar tendency in 1980s while examining the law and order situation. He observed

> ...public safety and security were issues tinged with an atmosphere of desperation that that had not been present 20 years earlier. The public was frightened and had lost faith in the ability of the government, particularly the police and courts to impose order' (Bayley 1983).

The situation in the last few years, instead of improving has deteriorated sharply. In some states the economically powerful section of the community uses private armies to maintain their privileged position. The killing of more than 60 people in one eastern state by the landed gentry's private army in spite of the fact that it was banned by the government in 1995 is one example.[65] Although not of the same magnitude, similar atrocities are known to have occurred in other states.

In large part this situation was created by the large parliamentary majority enjoyed by one political party until recently. Out of the twelve parliamentary elections until March 1998, the Congress party won eight. In the remaining three a coalition of opposition parties formed government, but lasted only 2.5 years (March 1977 to August 1979), 1.4 years (December 1989 to March 1991) and 1.7 years (May 1996 to December 1997) respectively (Government of India 1997). The defeat of the Congress party in the 1977 election was not due to any superior appeal of the opposition parties to the voters. It was a protest vote against Mrs Gandhi's emergency rule during which a significant

---

65 The *Statesman Weekly*, 1997. 'Caste, creed and carnage 13 December, Calcutta. Also see 'Rise and rise of private armies', by Naidu, C., in the *Hindusthan Times*, New Delhi, 14 December.

number of people suffered (particularly in the Hindi belt) due to the government's total disregard for human rights in pursuing, amongst other things, a coercive family planning program, dominance of non-elected persons in running the business of the government who had a close relationship with the people in power.

In the 1998 mid-term Parliamentary election, the right of the centre Bharatiya Janata Party (BJP) and its electoral allies won the largest number of seats, but was short of an absolute majority. Congress came second, well behind BJP and the Left United Front and its allies came third. The BJP, with the support of its allies has formed the government, but some of its allies constantly threaten to withhold their support.

The vast majority enjoyed by Congress since independence resulted in Parliament routinely rubber stamping executive decisions along party lines. This uninterrupted enjoyment of political power by one party, and the failure of other political parties to establish a credible alternative made the ruling party complacent and arrogant. As a result it started flouting the spirit of the constitutional provisions to suit its own objectives. Its inability to distinguish between what is permitted under the constitutional provisions as against what is good for the party became clear when one Congress minister claimed in the Parliament in 1975 that the Government reserved the right to function freely in its own sphere, implying that it would not be deterred by the spirit of the Constitutional provisions (Noorani 1984b). Similarly, another Congress minister stated in the Parliament in 1988 that the President can have only what government decides. In support of his argument he quoted Article 74 of the Constitution which was refuted by all constitutional experts as inappropriate (Noorani 1988).

The economic policies of the government, until the foreign exchange crisis of 1991, also contributed to strengthening the government's hand in ignoring or misinterpreting the Constitution to obtain undue advantage for the party. This was done by silencing or neutralising the economic and social forces which could effectively influence the political process to challenge such misuses by using its monopoly to issue licenses, distribute permits and so on. In this way it ensured loyalty from communities who benefited from maintaining such arrangements.

The power to appoint people in critical administrative positions also assisted governments in making their own interpretation of the constitutional provisions, and apply them wrongfully to meet their own objectives. Government used this power by appointing persons who would remain loyal to governments' wishes instead of giving full allegiance to the legal or constitutional provisions of their individual offices to which they were appointed. Migdal rightly concluded that this types of operational behaviour reflected a lack of confidence in state institutions (Migdal 1988:206–37), by noting that Mrs Gandhi moved loyal officials into key positions before declaring state of emergency.[66]

In addition, government's advantage in having a monopoly over the electronic media (until recently) was skillfully exploited to project its image often at the expense of the accuracy of the broadcast news. Furthermore, its absolute control over funds to place government advertisements, particularly in the vernacular print-media ensured that, at least in the majority of cases, the media followed the government line in news distribution. In a country where significant adult illiteracy exists, this power to provide funding support suited the government of the day very well. It is only very recently that the newly established Prasar Bharati Board has been chartered to function independently and maintain impartiality in news broadcasts.[67]

The frequent dismissal of state governments in violation of the expressed provisions in the constitution, withholding state legislative bills sent to the President for assent (one bill was found to be pending for more than eight years) and failure to give effective economic power to states only accelerated the loss of people's confidence in the constitutional process, and the ability of the government to govern, leading to uncertainty, fear and violence.

Thus in spite of the good intentions of framers of the constitution, no healthy constitutional convention had been established in India. Even in areas where constitutional provisions were clearly stipulated, application of those provisions has been messy and distorted. As the government became dominated by rent seekers, both the government and the bureaucracy failed to make a separation between the public and private spheres in social and economic life. In this environment implementing agencies exhibited a wide range of inappropriate

66 *Times of India,* 1977, 26 June, Mumbai. Quoted in Migdal (*Op. cit.*)
67 The *Statesman Weekly*, 1997. 'Prasar Bharati opens all files to public scrutiny', Calcutta, 29 November. Also see *The Hindusthan Times*, 'Gill(s) help Doordarshan breathe easy New Delhi', 1 December.

behaviour: executives who acted undemocratically, courts (in some instances at least) made unreasoned decisions and bureaucrats responded not to public but to private interests.

In addition to the failure of successive governments to apply the Constitution properly, the inadequacy of the Constitution itself to satisfy the country and community's requirements is clearly manifested in the large number of amendments made so far. More than 80 amendments have been made in 47 years of the Constitution's life. Normally, amendment of a constitution in a federal structure should not be an easy process. But in India amendment of the constitution in a number of categories is comparatively easy as reflected in the large number of amendments made so far.

The Indian Constitution can be amended in three different ways, depending upon the nature and type of the provision of the Constitution (Mukherjee and Mukherjee 1995:286–90). However, when one political party enjoyed majority in both houses of the Parliament and in most of the states, amending some provisions of the constitution, irrespective of whether there were urgent requirements to do so, became relatively easy.

Given that the implied federal provisions of the constitution have been largely ignored by the Central Government during the first five decades of the constitution's existence, that the centre-state relationship remains a major political issue for the country, that secessionist powers are stronger than ever before and given that political parties have not been able to guide people in developing a healthy political convention, it would be appropriate to consider whether India needs a new constitution to reflect all its aspirations and operational procedures more clearly and unequivocally than before.

A number of political commentators and constitutional experts have already questioned the relevance of a number of constitutional clauses in contemporary India. One such clause which has received enormous attention is clause 356 of the Constitution concerning the office of the Governor. One commentator argued that this office should be abolished, or at least regionalised, and that it should be elected by the concerned legislatures (Kaul 1997). There are other examples dealing with other clauses. This example is cited to emphasise that the Indian Constitution needs a fresh look, although many may think the idea abhorrent.

The Constitution is an important document for a country and should not be tinkered with easily or at the whim of the executive or legislature. However, in India's case it has been amended at regular intervals, and has also been misused in a number of cases for political expediency. As a result, instead of gaining the peoples' confidence, their faith in the political process which misused and wrongly interpreted many of the constitutional provisions has gradually eroded. In view of this it would be appropriate to examine whether a more prescriptive constitution to suit a multi-ethnic, multi-religious, multi-lingual country like India would restore peoples' faith in the constitution as something that could ensure the Parliament and executive's undiminished commitment to civil society and good governance values. This is more important today than ever before because with the changing political scene, as a coalition government is becoming a fact of life at the federal level and with different parties occupying state governments, amendments of constitutional provisions will increasingly become more difficult, irrespective of their appropriateness.

It is acknowledged that many will dismiss the idea of a new constitution as irresponsible and not required. Their argument perhaps will take the line that it is the people who make the constitution effective, and hence even a new constitution will not make much difference from the present situation until people change their perceptions and behavioural patterns with respect to government issues. While such an argument has a point, at the same time it should be acknowledged that more prescriptive provisions in the constitution would have prevented many of the questionable interpretations made by unscrupulous politicians which have led to the current widespread frustration.

The president of the Bar Association of India was right when on the 50th anniversary of India's independence said 'What we appear to have lost...is the sense of idealism that inspired the founding fathers of the Constitution' (Nariman 1998). While idealism can not be artificially transplanted, or constitutional provisions alone cannot fully prevent misuse of power by any arm of the state, a constitution which takes full cognisance of the social, economic and political realities in the country can create a better framework to assist in pursuing and preserving good governance, and civil society principles and values. After all, a constitution is written to suit the situation at the time of its drafting, and hence there should not be any reason why it could not be rewritten in significantly changed economic, social and political circumstances.

India's near neighbour, Thailand, which was never colonised, rewrote its constitution more than a dozen times to suit its own requirements, and India's former colonial ruler never had a written constitution. There is no golden rule for any constitution; it should be a document (or a firmly established convention) to guide the community in designing its own political and administrative structure. If the underlying conditions in a country change, the constitution should reflect the realities of the situation where contemporary values and aspirations find their rightful places, and not remain a static document.

Parliamentary Control

Currently, Parliament has hardly any effective mechanisms for undertaking a critical examination of the executive's work. Almost uninterrupted occupation of the treasury benches by one political party has partly contributed in Parliament's inability to exercise its full authority over the executive. Although there are a number of Parliamentary Consultative Committees to overview the functions of the executive, these Committees do not have any teeth, they can neither summon witnesses nor seek evidence under oath, nor can they demand the production of necessary files or documents before the Committee, or examine any official records. Given that the entire system has been manipulated by successive governments to fulfil their own agendas, some fundamental changes are necessary if Parliament is to become supreme in overseeing functions of the executive.

Ideally this situation can only be overcome by strong commitment by all political parties to make committees function with some degree of power. However, unprincipled political alliance during election times or post-election horse-trading to form a government are unlikely to assist in allowing consultative committees to function with real teeth. This will therefore require a more prescriptive approach to ensure that executive's performance is adequately monitored and examined by Parliament.

Establishing joint-parliamentary committees (JPCs) should be the first step in building this process. Joint Parliamentary Committees should be tasked to scrutinise the performance of government departments and ensure the community has the opportunity to effectively input into legislation put before the Parliament.

Joint Parliamentary Committees should be empowered to take evidence under oath from relevant officials, other interested organisations and parties, call for documents and files on relevant subjects while considering departmental budgets and their performances. If necessary, the Committee should be able to examine government officials in camera to ensure that sensitive matters remain confidential to the Committee alone. In addition, the Committee should be able to invite submissions from the public or summon witnesses, should it consider this important in examining departmental performances.

The executive privilege to withhold information from the committees should be rarely used, and only in exceptional circumstances. However, for a healthy democratic convention, it would be desirable that, at least, the chairpersons of committees, in such circumstances, are briefed about the nature of the information being withheld along with the reasons for such decision.

Furthermore, to encourage input from community organisations and interested individuals in legislation, Committees should sit in various regional centres all over the country. This will encourage community participation in government by signaling that the Parliament wants peoples' input in shaping the focus and content of the legislation. More importantly, it will establish that the Parliament is not out of touch with the ordinary people and is genuinely eager to assist institution building by establishing community confidence in the virtues of a civil society where everybody has an opportunity to contribute, should they desire.

Under this arrangement every government department will be required by law to submit an annual report through their minister for Parliament's scrutiny, and the Committee should be required to examine these reports thoroughly before submitting its findings to the Parliament within a set time period. The minister responsible should be required to respond to the Committee findings including the steps taken by the department to overcome any policy failures or administrative lapses, as may be identified by the Committee. The departmental head will be required to personally take responsibility for the contents in the annual report. It should include all aspects of departmental operations including policy, budget, staffing matters, future direction and its role in servicing the government and the public.

This mechanism will force the bureaucracy to pursue a disciplined path and justify their existence as they are funded by the scarce public resources. It will also enable the government of the day to demand from the bureaucracy that its policies are appropriately executed. At the same time the bureaucracy will be aware that it cannot neglect to perform, otherwise both Parliament and the public will have the capacity to censure them through these Committees which will not only give them a bad name, but may put them in a position detrimental to their Minister's and department's interests.

The current administrative practices do not allow detailed scrutiny of the performance of the bureaucracy and their departments. This often means that spectacular failures on the bureaucracy's part virtually remain uncensored, with no guarantee that such failures would not reoccur. Their failures often could be catastrophic for the country and its citizens. A clear example of such recent failure was the bureaucracy's inability to effectively warn government about the fiscal crisis India faced in 1991 (Bhagwati 1995:72).

The JPCs should operate as a watch dog with their own secretarial support. The committee members will be expected to operate on a bipartisan basis and their political allegiance should not dominate the committee proceedings and reports. As far as practicable committee hearings should be open. An open process will improve peoples' confidence in the constitutional and democratic process of government. The membership of the Committees should be equally divided between the treasury and the opposition benches with the Chairperson having a casting vote and individual members with the right to submit dissenting reports. The Chair of the Committees should be equally divided between the government and the opposition between various committees. To ensure that the basic structure of the Committee remains unchanged throughout the life of a Parliament, should a member of the committee shift political allegiance, the member should resign from the Committee to ensure that balance between the government and the opposition is maintained.

To restore peoples' confidence in the Parliament and its capacity to oversee the functions of government, this mechanism should be given priority consideration both by the Government and the Parliament. It may be asked what guarantee is there that the system will assist institution building and bring back the community's confidence in the government and the state machinery? There are two reasons for optimism

- the Committee will have virtually unlimited power to seek information on all aspects of departmental operation under the watchful eye of both government and the opposition; and
- by inviting public submissions and conducting public hearings on new legislation at regional centres, it will be able to get people involved in the law making process and the government, which after all is owned by the community.

Another important area which requires Parliamentary control is the power to recommend for appointment and overview the functions of a limited number of key government functionaries. Bipartisan support would assist office holders in the key functionaries to discharge their responsibilities with the added assurance that they have the support of the highest institution in the land when facing undue political or other pressures that might be put on them to overlook lawful provisions which might adversely effect the interests of powerful groups or persons in government and the community. Experiences in both developed and developing countries indicate that occupants of these positions remain vulnerable to political pressures to favour person or persons in critical financial or legal matters. This bipartisan Parliamentary support will strengthen their capacity to perform with full knowledge that their performance will be publicly evaluated and their positions protected by the highest body in the land, the Parliament.

All these positions are to be classified as statutory positions, although formal appointment will be made by the government of the day at the recommendation of the Parliament. A committee of the Parliament will consider all names received by it through invitation or through open advertisement and recommend a panel of names (say three) to the government for its consideration. The Committee should act as a vetting agency primarily focussing on applicants' integrity and managerial record, and not issues which cannot be considered relevant to the job. This stipulation is required to ensure that the Committee deliberations do not follow the American practice of becoming a star chamber, often focussing on unrelated issues, not relevant to the job requirements. Should the government find any of the names recommended unacceptable, it should provide its reasons in writing. In such an event the process will start again and this time the government will be obliged to appoint from the panel of names recommended by the committee. This process will ensure that persons with impeccable credentials and strong records of independence are appointed to these offices.

The suggested positions are

- Central Revenue Board: responsible for administering government's taxation policies including customs and excise duties
- Election Commission: responsible for all matters relevant to conducting Parliamentary and State elections
- Auditor and Comptroller General: responsible for ensuring that public funds are expended with the full authority of the legislature, and all expenditures are incurred diligently and efficiently
- Corporate regulating agency: responsible for overseeing and policing the operational practices of the corporate sector
- Director of Public Prosecution: responsible for deciding, on receipt of investigation reports, whether formal charges will be laid on the available evidence put to it or if further investigation is required
- Chief Statistician: responsible for all aspects of economic, demography and social data for policy development purposes at all levels of the government, and for public use
- Ombudsman (Lokpal): responsible for investigating complaints made against a government department or agency by ordinary citizens of the country
- Human Rights Commission: responsible for ensuring that rights granted by the Constitution and international protocols and covenants agreed to by the Government are properly applied
- Independent Broadcasting Control Authority: responsible for managing publicly owned broadcasting facilities to ensure that all publicly owned broadcasting facilities operate independent of the executive arm of the government in line with their charters as approved by the Parliament
- A new crime and corruption control authority which will incorporate within it the existing vigilance commission: this body will be responsible for monitoring, and investigating corrupt and criminal behaviour of all public officials including

public servants of section head and above level, and the federal law enforcement agencies.

These agencies should be established under separate laws of the Parliament and remain autonomous. Appointments to Boards and of the Chief Executive should not be necessarily from the ranks of civil service alone. These positions will be open to everybody, the sole criterion being the best person available to perform the tasks required of the position. The person should have a proven track record in his/her field of expertise including highest level of managerial capacity and impeccable integrity that should be able to command community respect.

All appointments in these positions should be for a seven year term, and appointees can only be removed by the President on a resolution of the Parliament on proven grounds of incompetence or gross impropriety which might erode community confidence in the office. The President will have the right to seek clarifications on issues covered by the resolution. Reasons for seeking clarification should be given in writing to ensure that everything is above board.

Many Parliamentarians may not agree with this provision, as it may be seen as restricting the capacity of the Parliament to perform its duties. The suggested mechanism will assist in maintaining the integrity of the office and will protect it from any perceived bias of the Parliament, because the office might have questioned some of the practices followed or benefits enjoyed by the Parliamentarians in violation of the established rules and practices. Even in Britain, the birthplace of the Westminster system the Monarch's role is not mechanical. The former British Prime Minister Sir Harold Wilson in an interview said that for centuries a key element of Britain's unwritten constitution is for the Monarch to advise, to encourage and to warn (Wilson 1982).

All appointees should be eligible for appointment to a second term. A seven year term will ensure that the appointment for second term will be considered by a different Parliament and scrutinised by a body which was not responsible for the original recommendation. Their salaries and conditions of appointment will be set by the Parliament at the time of each individual appointment. This is important because often to obtain the services of the right person, fiscal compensation may have to be paid to attract them from outside the service. For example, the Director of Public Prosecution has to be a highly successful lawyer with impeccable integrity. To attract such a person from the Bar would require that the person was adequately compensated for the loss of income which he or she would have to forgo by accepting the position. By ensuring a proper remuneration package (within the country's overall socioeconomic context), the honesty and integrity of the position is highly likely to be maintained.

Appointees will submit their annual reports to the Parliament, although they will be required to be guided by the official government policies and provisions of laws of the country which might impact on their operation. Their function will be limited to executing government policy, and in the event of their inability to pursue any aspect of a policy they will be required to give in writing reasons for such failure. The administration of each of these agencies will remain the sole responsibility of the head of the agency and the relevant board who will be guided by government policies on all aspects of administration, unless otherwise specifically directed by the Parliament. (Further comments on each of the proposed positions are in Appendix Two).

Public Service and Public Sector Reform

Quality of management is key to the success or failure of any business enterprise. Management of state affairs is no different from managing a business. It is more complicated than a business enterprise because states and governments are obliged to look after the interests of the entire community, whereas the primary responsibility of the management in business is looking after its shareholders' interests. Post-independence administration is required to be more people and development focussed. Regrettably, the Indian bureaucracy has not been able to fulfil community expectations on both these areas. There are number of reasons for this failure.

India's situation is not much different from other newly independent Asian/African states, except that in pre-independence days the Indian bureaucracy was considered to be one of the best amongst the colonies. Generally speaking research undertaken by independent scholars confirms that third world bureaucracies, far from favouring the people they are required to serve, often systematically implement laws in ways that strengthen their own positions and those of the privileged in society. This has resulted in a great number of resentful and impoverished rural people, and a small minority with quantities of wealth (Davidson 1992).

However, within this broad similarity there exists one major difference between bureaucracies in India and other developing countries. The Indian bureaucracy as a class has existed for a long time. The recruitment process from the early colonial days ensured that none but the élite could gain entry to the senior service. During the pre-independence days they cut their own niche to maintain their power base within the government. At that time the European collectors had to leave much of the management of their districts to their Indian junior officials, who often manipulated the system to their own advantage and enrichment (Marshall 1997). By maintaining the basic structure of the pre-independent bureaucracy, the government did not assist its cause of promoting the development of organisations to meet the needs of the masses, who mostly lived in rural areas. Nehru, who was the head of the post-independent government for more than one and a half decades, admitted that one of his major failures was not to have changed the bureaucratic apparatus which was established by the British after independence (Subramaniam 1992:24). Researchers confirm this failure. While examining the powers of Indian bureaucrats, Potter found that Indian revolutionaries (freedom fighters who formed the government in the post-colonial period) perhaps tended to underestimate the strength of the state bureaucracy (Potter 1986).

Bureaucratic failure in other countries, particularly in Africa, was due to totally different reasons, although in recent years some similarity is noticeable. Following independence, when Africanisation of the bureaucracy commenced the reason became clear. In post-colonial Africa there were two public realms: a *primordia* public realm, governed by *primordial* groupings, ties and sentiments and a colonial-derived 'civic' public realm. Most educated Africans are members of both these public realms (Ekeh 1975). This duality often precludes impartial and effective application of government's declared policies. Although it has no direct relevance in India, the underlying factor remains somewhat similar for some sections of the Indian bureaucracy. Conflicts arise as many senior positions are reserved for the socially underprivileged class in the community. This artificial division injects a tendency to partisanship among all groups of officials, although nobody will admit to it. This issue requires an unbiased examination in a non-emotive way.

The Indian constitution has made provisions under Articles 15(4) and 16(4) to reserve certain number of government posts for scheduled casts and scheduled tribes. Given the economically and socially backward position of the members of these communities, it is difficult to argue against these provisions. However, it is questionable that if efficiency is the sole criteria for appointment then whether there are alternatives options available to uplift their economic and social conditions without affecting the quality of the recruitment. Pursuance of such special provisions in perpetuity is likely to cause friction, and has the potential to damage the integrity of the service and fabric of the society (Ray 1995).

This division is not helpful in the long run interest of the service either. First, it creates animosity between those who joined the service under open conditions and those who were selected under the reservation criteria. Second, by keeping this division in perpetuity a sub-culture is preserved which tend to work in similar lines as found in the *primordial* public realm and *primordial* groupings, ties and sentiments in many of the African states. Finally, the very existence of discriminatory policy on cast or tribal basis act against genuine upliftment of the underprivileged class as the system itself perpetuates an 'us and them' mentality.

The schedule cast population constituted 16.48 per cent of the total population in 1991 and they held 16.9 per cent of the central government positions. In Group A of the public service their representation was 10.24 per cent, in Group B 12.6 per cent, in Group C 15.73, in Group D 20.46 per cent, and about 50 per cent in the sweeper category. In the scheduled tribe category—which constitutes 8.08 per cent of India's population—only 5.48 per cent of the positions were held by them. Their distribution in various groups was 2.9 per cent, 2.8 per cent, 5.4 per cent, 6.2 and 6.9 per cent respectively (Government of India 1996:184–95). The figures clearly show that the former group is yet to reach high level positions proportionate to their number. The second group has not yet secured proportionate employment in any of the groups.

It is argued that the best way to raise the social and economic conditions of the disadvantaged group is by providing assistance, and economic and institutional support to build their capacity to compete at par, instead of negative approach through quotas and reservations. Because of the entrenched disadvantage, if a negative approach is required such policies should have a sun set clause so that every body knows that in the long-run no body will be disadvantaged. The underlying tension in many Indian states owe their origin to this policy.

A two step action is required to ensure that both these groups receive assistance to uplift their economic and social positions. Firstly, generous assistance should be provided to the people in these groups based on the criteria of affordability, instead of the current practice of favouring on the basis of one's birth alone. Assistance should include family support as well to encourage vertical social mobility of the group because in many instances economic reasons prevent children from these families pursuing a non-traditional vocation outside their social group. Providing direct financial and related support for a reasonable period of time would help to prepare them to compete openly for those positions which are now reserved for them.

This mechanism will also enable them to earn their pride which will assist individual and group confidence to rise, will assist in increasing the authority of the occupant of the position and any simmering undercurrent of discontent will be defused. Current artificial divisions which have the potential to create inefficiencies and friction within the administration and undermine the effectiveness of government policies will be removed through refocusing policy directions. Within this context, those who are economically well off within these groups should not be able to seek special dispensation simply because of their caste or tribe. Given that many anti-poverty programs targeted to uplift the economic and social standard of these two groups are not found to be effective, the most likely reason for such failures is that the economically weaker in the group are not accessing the benefits of such programs.

It will take time before the suggested policy reforms enable the affected community to feel confident to compete on its own ability. It will therefore be necessary to keep the current policy of reservation, but a sun set clause should be introduced to signal to the community that this reservation policy is only a temporary measure. For the long-term interest of the country, this special dispensation is required as an interim measure, and in the medium to long-term time frame all appointments will be made on grounds of efficiency alone. In public administration the right signals can avoid conflicts in the long-run. There can be no doubt that creating capacities to compete economically and professionally is a more potent tool for uplifting social status than reservation policies will ever be.

Electoral Reform

The growth of regional political parties and mushrooming of new political parties all over India (often led by persons who only have self-interest at heart) not only creates confusion in the minds of the electorate but creates an uncertainty on the outcome of the election. The 1998 Parliamentary election was contested by seven national and 34 state or regional political parties recognised by the Election Commission. In addition, a large number of single issue local political parties and independent candidates also contested the election.[68]

With only about one half of the eligible voters literate and a significant number of them living below the poverty line, having a large number of political parties with competing slogans, and rarely with articulated policies creates confusion in the voters' mind. It also creates an environment where voters become gullible to threats by powerful forces of various nature. In many electorates it is well known that to disregard the dictates of political muscle men could invite trouble in the post election period. In one such case almost entire population of a village was wiped out by political hoodlums for ignoring the dictates of a locally powerful organisation.[69] This is not an isolated case. The Government's decision to deploy 700 companies of central para-military forces to supplement local and state law-enforcement on poll duty in 1998 along with the decision to deploy the Border Security Force, if required, highlights the problem.[70] If nothing else, this indicates that there is something fundamentally wrong with how the constitutional provisions are working, and how people are relating to these provisions and their relationship with the government and the administration.

It is not possible to fight disruptive elements by law enforcement agencies alone. In many instances law enforcement agencies' performance leaves a lot to be desired. Eventually, community involvement and cooperation is essential in efforts to fight these disruptive elements. But to do so, there needs to be an environment which provides the community with the confidence to extend their cooperation. Good governance practices can provide this environment.

---

68 The *Economic Times*, 1998. New Delhi, 17 January.

69 The *Statesman Weekly*, 1998. 'Fear of reprisal prevents free ballot', Calcutta, 7 February.

70 The *Economic Times*, 1998. New Delhi, 17 January.

In this context some current election practices need to be modified to create a better environment where the ordinary citizens can feel confident of acting on their own initiative, and at the same time also improve the election process to make it less confusing for the people to elect a representative of their own choice without any pressure being put on them.

From the reaction of ordinary voters it is apparent that although the election environment has improved significantly during the last two parliamentary elections, there remains a significant scope for improving the representation and the election process. The following measures will contribute to improving the current situation further.

- Nominations of candidates must be supported by a certain number of eligible voters of a constituency so that dummy candidates cannot be put up easily by unscrupulous parties to split vote on religious, caste or ethnic grounds. In the Parliamentary election it could be some 350 voters (based on 50 voters from each of the assembly constituency covered by a parliamentary constituency). It is a well known practice that to split opposition vote often many candidates adopt this path, should a candidate feel that votes from a particular group of people would not favour him/her. Persons should not be eligible to nominate more than one candidate, should not receive any financial inducement for nominating a candidate nor should be asked by anybody else other than the candidate to support the nomination. This will make the election process a bit more complex, but to get a proper representation the complexity is worth adopting. Sponsoring candidates and providing logistic support to candidates with the intention of splitting the opposition vote should be considered a criminal offence.
- Currently many politicians do not bother to serve their constituency because they can stand from as many constituencies as they wish. This not only makes mockery of representing a particular constituency, but also requires new elections if a candidate is elected from more than one constituency. There is no reason why tax payers' money should be spent because a particular candidate was not sure whether he/she should be elected from a particular constituency. Therefore, no person should be allowed to stand from two constituencies, and no person should be allowed to stand in an election if he or she remains a member of any other legislature

in the country. This will force political parties to put up serious candidates, and not take a chance with a particular electorate.

- The current provision of people joining the ministry without being elected for the first six months should be scrapped. This will reduce the scope for manipulation by political parties or corrupt leadership to nominate people to become minister at the expense of those who have already earned peoples' confidence by getting duly elected in the legislature. During the last fifty years there have been a number of cases when party machines or powerful individual leadership got people (a fair description would be people from their own group to maintain their power base) into particular ministerial positions and then got them elected at a later date. There is nothing wrong in this process if it were used for getting outstanding persons into the ministry. However, in India often it has been misused to the detriment of the community interest. Because of this it would be better to stop this practice altogether. If political parties are keen to get certain outstanding person in the ministry, they should ensure that they are elected in the legislature first.
- Barring candidates with criminal records from contesting an election is a more complex issue than it appears on the surface for two reasons. First, concerning the definition of criminality, there exists some ambiguity. For example, many of India's independence fighters would be considered criminal if Britain was still ruling India, and one of the most celebrated of the international criminals would be President Mandela. In other worlds some criminal activities have very significant political overtones, and the issue needs to be carefully addressed. Second, just being accused of a criminal offence does not necessarily mean that the person is guilty. Given that in India it often takes years for a case to be heard and adjudicated there is no guarantee that a person will not be unduly debarred from contesting an election. The Election Commission and the political parties in particular need to give further thought to how to handle this situation. One option could be to have a small board within the Election Commission consisting of eminent jurists to vet in a non-legalistic way the nominations of those who have been charged with criminal offence. If in their opinion there exists a realistic chance of the person being acquitted of the charges then the person will be allowed to contest the election, and otherwise

not. Political parties may also decide not to take the risk of nominating such candidates.

- To deny identification of voters' preferences for any particular candidate, all votes cast in a constituency may be pooled together before counting commences. In this way whether a particular area within the constituency voted for a particular candidate cannot be identified. This will reduce the chances of any reprisals being mounted by disgruntled candidates. This is not an ideal solution, but at least will assist in improving electorates' confidence that they can cast their vote according to their own choice.
- Electoral recognition of political parties should only be given after public scrutiny and hearing. It should be a semi-judicial process which should include public examination of issues such as objectives, financial resources and support base before recognition is granted. Should there be serious public objections raised against a proposed party relating to its aims, objectives or administrative procedures, recognition should be denied. While introducing such measures procedures must be such as to provide absolute confidence that the power of the Commission can never be misused by any particular group for political gains.
- Past experience indicates that often small groups or powerful individuals try to form a political party shortly before an election when they fail to extract the advantage they thought they could from their former party or previous associates. This situation could be overcome by a simple clause that for electoral recognition, a political party must be in existence as a recognised political party for at least 12 months before the official declaration of the election date. This will also make the Election Commission's task easier and should assist it in avoiding any controversy over its decisions.

Social Awareness

In any administrative system the community is the biggest stake holder and hence their involvement in understanding and executing changes is vital. A significant amount of work therefore is required to educate, appraise and involve the community in this effort. To achieve this there exists an urgent need to engage in social engineering with effective and clearly visible policies and programs.

This social engineering process should commence by introducing at various stages targeted education programs outlining what government administration does, how it affects communities and how communities can interact with this process. Alongside this, the values of a civil society and good governance practices in nation building should be highlighted. The major impediments to civil society should be identified, and communities should be encouraged with appropriately targeted programs to remove those impediments for the benefit of the community and the nation. These tasks are not easy. All education programs should be specifically designed to meet the needs of clearly identified individual groups, because the absorption capacity of all groups may not be the same. Furthermore, all programs should be pilot-tested before they are executed and results evaluated to ensure that the programs are attaining their objectives. It should be a continuous process, and be considered as a part of the overall social and community development program. Most importantly, the social engineering process should not be taken lightly or casually.

One of the best ways to engage communities in understanding their problems and articulating these issues is to get them access to the air-waves. Television services are no longer monopolised by the government as people have access to other channels. This has opened up the electronic media to uncontrolled news broadcasts and provided opportunities for open public debate on important issues. This is however not the case with radio as yet. As nearly half of the adult population is illiterate, the role of print media remains limited in engaging wider communities to articulate their concerns or propagate their views widely. To encourage people to engage in informed debate on issues of concern to them and that impact on their daily lives, the airwaves can be very effectively used. Currently air broadcasts are mostly from the capital cities and in spite of some efforts they cannot engage wider communities in their deliberations. The government therefore should give serious consideration to issuing radio broadcast licenses on a sub-regional basis whereby communities can own and operate radio stations with direct input in program development and broadcast policy. This will encourage people to get directly involved in the governance process, assist in promoting civil society values and crystallise issues which the government may not always be aware or even understand their importance to the local community. The only caveat should be that the ownership of such radio stations remain broadly community based within the region for which the license is granted. This is particularly important to ensure that ownership of stations does not fall into the hands of powerful individuals or segments of the community who might use the stations for self-seeking purposes; it can be ensured by stringent ownership and operational guidelines.

Some General Issues

Institutional changes are always difficult to achieve and it is a slow process, it requires commitment from all parties—political parties, the government, bureaucracy and the community at large. There is a natural tendency to resist changes in an environment of fear and uncertainty. The Indian bureaucracy in its present form is more than 100 years old and is fully entrenched in an administrative system which is basically insular in nature. This inhibits them from reshaping and redesigning the government and the administrative structure in any radical way.

The absence of any radical changes in the administrative structure and procedures following independence, demands created by the global political and economic changes, and the technological revolution make it immensely urgent that fundamental changes in the administration are made. At the same time there exists genuine concern among those who will be adversely affected by any radical change and hence their reluctance to initiate, introduce or accept changes easily. However, without any fundamental shifts in the policy making process, resource allocation within the government and between governments, government financial accounting practices and procedures, many of the current failures in the administrative system cannot be rectified. These reforms are essential if India's development efforts are to generate momentum and rejuvenate community spirit, making people feel that their involvement is important to sustained development.

Specific actions required to introduce major changes should therefore be taken simultaneously on four fronts. First, as suggested earlier, a critical look at the Constitution is required with a view either to radically modifying it or drafting a new constitution to meet the challenges of the next millennium. This will not be an easy task and will perhaps take years to arrive at a consensus on any remodelled constitution. But this issue needs to be on the table and must be debated vigorously with an open mind and clear understanding of India's current and future needs, aspirations and how best they can be achieved. The failures of the last fifty years will set the agenda and will assist in crystallising future needs. One important focus has to be clear delineation of the functions and responsibilities of the three tiers of government within a federal structure.

The current delineation of functions is neither here nor there, providing fertile ground for inefficiency and friction. Many of the centre-state relationship issues have already been dealt with by the Sarkaria Commission. These need to be revisited and modified where appropriate. On the relationship between state and local-self governments, detailed investigations need to be carried out to establish a most cost-effective mechanism to deliver services, and more importantly to avoid duplication. The 73rd and 74th Amendments of the Constitution in 1992 provide for the local self-government at the village and town levels. However, their effectiveness remains doubtful because as it stands it is just another layer of government without clear delineation of its functional, revenue raising and expenditure responsibilities.

While there has been a lot of fanfare about the effectiveness of the third tier of government, in effect it is just another layer of government and far from effective delineation of power and responsibility to local communities. There is already a significant amount of criticism that the third layer has effectively decentralised the inefficiency and corruption which have been rampant in other two tiers of government.[71]

Instead of divesting full responsibilities to district boards, some states are engaged in maintaining their authority through the back door in the name of maintaining prescribed technical standards of projects. This is done by sending state officials on special duty to the *zilla parishad* (district boards). If state governments are genuinely motivated to divest development responsibilities and power at the grass roots level, it would be more appropriate for them to set the standards and make it a requirement for district boards to perform accordingly, and leave administrative and management matters to them. This process would not only be cost-effective, but it would avoid the problem of serving

---

71 De, N., 1997; A well known management expert in an article in *Bartaman*, a metropolitan vernacular daily, on 31 July, discusses how various state governments have been violating the constitutional provisions, and are maintaining their control on local government bodies and *panchayets* by dubious means. He further asserts that these bodies in most cases have become a fertile ground for corrupt practices by respective ruling state governments, irrespective of their political colour.

two masters currently faced by the Indian Administrative Service Officers. Local self-government, everywhere in the world, is considered a grass-roots organisation; people need to be appropriately trained to manage these bodies efficiently. By sending generalist service-officials to serve two masters (district boards and the state governments simultaneously), all the current inefficiencies of the administrative set-up will be maintained and communities will never learn to take responsibility for their own actions.

Second, while it will take time to examine the constitutional issues appropriately, administrative reform can be undertaken immediately with a view to simplifying procedures, improving accountability and dismantling monopoly situations wherever they exist within the government. It is recognised that the existing situation is cumbersome and complicated, and vested interests are so entrenched that internally generated improvements and modifications will be unlikely to achieve any fundamental shift within the system. It is no fault of any individual; it is a structural deficiency and similar situations can be found in other countries. The task therefore will neither be simple nor easy.

Third, improvements in fiscal management including the compulsory introduction of modern accounting practices to reflect the true financial situation of governments must be a priority in any reform initiative. There are many examples which clearly indicate that expenditures are incurred without transparent justifications to satisfy political needs of the party in power or to seek favour from sections of the community without parliamentary approval. In most such cases, the executive power was used in incurring such expenses. Stringent financial discipline will force governments and the bureaucracy to ensure that policy objectives are achieved, principles of efficiency while allocating public resources are strictly followed and discretionary power to justify public expenditure is brought to minimum.

Currently ministers use their discretionary powers in many cases to avoid parliamentary scrutiny of such expenditure thus subverting parliamentary accountability in such matters. More importantly, economic or social justifications of such expenditure will never be known or cannot be scrutinised. For example, in 1997 the Minister for Railways approved benefits to railway porters although they were not directly employed by the railways. Similarly the minister issued a large number of complementary railway passes to selected groups of people without any public scrutiny of the process. Subsequently, on receipt of a public interest petition, the Delhi High Court instructed the railway authorities to submit certain documents to the court for examination. Similar practices have been continuing in many other areas of the government. To stop such abuses discretionary powers should only be rarely used—any such expenditure should be costed and these costings must be available for public scrutiny. Failure to do so will encourage corrupt practice, and make people loose faith in the impartiality of the administration.

Governments should also be required to immediately adopt accrual accounting process for budgetary purposes. Current accounting practices hardly make it possible to obtain accurate financial information on government expenditures and their future liability on financial decisions taken today. Many of the governments' decisions imply a long-term expenditure commitment, the magnitude of which cannot be known unless total liability is costed. Private sector business is run on the basis of total income and total liability. Governments also need to know what their total liability would be for each of their expenditure decisions. For example, in the last decade (1988/89 to 1996/97) combined revenue expenditure of the central and state governments increased by 201 per cent, compared to 235 per cent in administrative services expenditures and 284 per cent in pension payment for public servants and allied workers for whom pensions are paid from the public exchequer (World Bank 1997c:92–3). Funds required for future pension payments (which currently remain unfunded), if overseas experience is any guide, will increase exponentially as peoples' longevity increases. Unless governments, both at the central and state levels, give urgent attention to this issue, pressures on future government budgets and taxpayers will be enormous. Governments must therefore ensure that future pension commitments are appropriately funded.

Fourth, a task force should be established, totally independent of the existing government and the bureaucracy, with the responsibility to radically redesign the public sector to meet India's needs in the first decades of the next millennium. It should examine the appropriateness of the existing system along with the standards set by international bench marks and practices, and where appropriate suggest new structure and new system. The task-force has to approach its task with an open mind, but must be determined to look anew on the whole issue of a cost-effective independent development administration without being unduly influenced by any section of the community. The work will require patience, determination and an understanding of the rapidly changing environment in which the public sector is and will be required to operate in the coming decades. The members of this task force therefore have to be chosen very carefully.

Last but not least, all reform measures should be based on the following principles: efficiency, accountability, predictability, openness and the supremacy of the rule of law.

Chapter Five: Conclusions

It is clear that in spite of its significant success in food production and exporting educated labour overseas in large numbers, India's overall development efforts have been significantly deficient. After 50 years of independence and nation building, nearly one third of its population lives below the poverty line, nearly one half of its adult population is illiterate and violence is widespread indicating a gradual loss of faith in the political process' ability to solve community problems and meet their aspirations. Above all rampant corruption at all levels indicates that the task ahead is very hard.

In such an environment simultaneous policy initiatives are required to achieve a high rate of economic growth and development to restore the already damaged social fabric in its pre-eminent position. Policy initiatives alone will not be adequate to achieve the objectives. These initiatives need to be sustained and must be practical and acceptable to the communities. This would require community involvement in the policy development and implementation process, and must be transparent, predictable and uniformly applicable. India needs to remember and understand that with the abolition of the cold war, if it cannot put its house in order nobody is going to stand by her in times of need. On the contrary, as it should have learned by now there are many forces both within and without who will take every opportunity to benefit by seeing that India remains weak and in an economic backwater.

India's near neighbour, China, and other Southeast Asian countries (until the recent economic collapse) have achieved a higher rate of economic growth and overall development during the last two decades. Following the recent economic crisis and with the stringent economic and administrative reform measures forced on them by international agencies, many of these countries can be expected to become economically and politically stronger in coming years. Should India aspire to match their growth and development rates she will have to redouble her efforts. Furthermore, if the income gap between India and other developed countries is to be reduced, India's growth rate has to be significantly higher than theirs. Failure to do so would only widen the gap and increase the community's frustration.

Constitutional reform should be considered a priority for India. The failures of the last five decades provide the justification for major reforms in this area, although constitutional reform on its own will not be adequate to achieve higher growth and development. It will only assist in creating a better environment for policy initiatives and program implementation. Given the magnitude of the problem, it would be useful to consider whether a new constitution would serve the country better. The Indian Constitution has already recorded more than 80 amendments in 48 years which indicates that it has failed to serve its purpose adequately. Moreover, by making so many amendments over such a short period the organic structure of the constitution is bound to have weakened. The constitution is a total document and when individual parts are amended frequently, the impact of these amendments on the remaining parts may dilute the overall strength and objectives of the constitution. It is therefore strongly suggested that on the available evidence, India should consider drafting a new constitution to meet its needs in the coming millennium.

India is a parliamentary democracy and its administrative structure is based on this. However, experience so far indicates that effective parliamentary control on the executive has been virtually non-existent. There are a number of reasons for this failure. It is essential that parliamentary control be reinforced if parliamentary democracy is to be effective in India. Reinforcing parliament's supremacy over the executive should be given priority.

Not many countries could sustain an economic growth rate of eight per cent or more for a long period of time. India would need to achieve economic growth of that magnitude for many years if it were to reduce its income gap with developed economies and some developing countries such as China. India therefore must also give high priority to developing an effective population policy. Unless this is given top most priority the economic, environmental and social consequences of the current population growth rate will be severe. Without a focused and effective population policy, whatever economic growth is achieved will be eaten away by a rapidly rising population.

It is reported that the Ninth five-year plan will focus on agriculture. However, one should not forget that world commodity prices remain most uncertain and vulnerable to wild fluctuations, and hence agricultural growth on its own will not be adequate to improve India's relative economic position. Furthermore, within the global economic context, the traditional focus on manufacturing and financial sectors will not generate enough employment to absorb the rapidly increasing labour force. It is therefore extremely important to specifically focus on the growth of self-employment and development of small-scale enterprises as an engine room for economic growth. Government policies and programs must be specifically focused to assist this sector as best as circumstances permit. It will require government to focus on four specific areas.

- Human resources: training individuals in basic business skills which would assist individuals to organise and run their own businesses. The current practice of producing graduates for clerical jobs should be discarded, because this does not prepare people to venture into economic activities.
- Technological assistance should be provided to those who require it to develop small enterprise skills. In providing technological assistance economic and technical sustainability should be a major consideration.
- Providing funding assistance to individuals within transparent and realistic guidelines.
- Provision of information on all aspects of business. Information is vital for the success of small enterprises who would not be able to succeed at the individual level. Professional organisations should be encouraged to venture in this field and assist those who come within their purview.

In this connection it is interesting to note that the Asia Pacific Economic Community (APEC) which India is trying to join expects the economic policies of their member countries to follow this line. The APEC Ministerial Council in its Osaka meeting in 1994 adopted these four points.[72]

In managing the economy, principles of accountability and transparency in policy decisions must be vigorously followed and implemented. All loss making agencies should be shut down, if necessary by paying compensation to all incumbent employees including substantial retraining facilities for them to re-enter the labour market, should they desire to do so. This will remove them from the governments' policy agenda and ensure they no longer bleed the public exchequer. If subsidies are warranted to achieve social policy objectives, they should be clearly identified and accounted for and they should be incorporated within the policy frame, which will assist in clearly identifying policy focus and better resource allocation.

72 *Financial Review,* 1994. Sydney, 25 October.

Reform measures will take a long time to be fully effective and bear fruit, but in a rapidly changing world time is an important element. In view of this, immediate measures should be taken to redesign the administrative structure. The following are suggested as a short to medium term measures for immediate administrative reform.

- Bureaucracy's role in the development administration, including their responsibilities and relationship with the government should be clearly identified. Bureaucracy's duel role should be to provide policy advice to the government and to execute government policies. The existing public service legislation should be totally remodeled to reflect these roles clearly and unambiguously. All regulations concerning public service focus and management should be kept simple and concise in order for everybody to understand them clearly. At operational levels the following should be made clear to all service personnel and the community so that everybody understands their responsibilities.

  a) All officials will be required to comply with Acts, Regulations and Statues, and any violation of these should be a chargeable offence without exception. This will prevent any illegal nexus developing between the bureaucracy and corrupt elements at all levels including politicians and business;

  b) The administration will be required to be sensitive to the public's needs, rights and aspirations and provide reasonable assistance to them in their dealings with the government and the service. Failure to do so may lead to disciplinary actions and payment of compensation if their actions cause any damage, financial or otherwise; and

  c) The public service should take responsibility for its decisions and ensure that they can be publicly defended within the existing laws, practices and conventions.

Responsibility for management of departments should be vested in departmental heads under clearly established, unambiguous guidelines and proper safeguards so that the power cannot be misused. This will assist in reducing the nexus between politicians and bureaucrats, which in the past has led to corruption, inefficiency and a self-seeking attitude at all levels. Some sections of the bureaucracy are all too aware of this nexus and are keen to ensure that the service is overhauled. In 1995 eight central government secretaries (administrative heads of central ministries) and 10 state chief secretaries (administrative head of state governments) asked the then prime minister to overhaul the service.[73] And yet no concrete steps have been taken to address any of the fundamental issues they raised.

Government should be responsible for appointing heads of departments only; all other recruitments should be openly conducted by a service-wide independent selection committee and the departmental heads should take responsibility for appointing officials on the recommendation of the selection committee. The selection criteria for each position should be publicly available, and neutral so as not to favour any section of the community or the service.

The decision making process should be decentralised with clear and enforceable guidelines; administration should be required to place emphasis on outcomes rather than the process. Public service guidelines should emphasise team work instead of maintaining a rigid hierarchical system, and staff should be required to take responsibility for decisions taken, and not hide behind rigid rules and regulations.

Cost effectiveness in policy options and program delivery should be considered as part of the performance of departments and their executives. Departments will be required to divest public sector functions that other sectors can do better in economic and effectiveness terms. Many of the service delivery functions can be handed over to community organisations or in some cases private organisations with a pre-determined performance bench mark. Departments will therefore be required to justify their functions at regular intervals, preferably during the budget process. They should also be required to clearly identify reasons for their existence and prepare bench marks against which their performance will be measured.

Examination of the structure of one state department revealed that it had 100 senior executive officers. Compared to any developed country's structure, this is overwhelmingly top heavy. Serious consideration should be given to reducing such top heavy structures by 50 per cent at least at the initial stage, subject to further detailed examination of departmental functions. If overseas experience is any guide, this reduction will hardly impact on departmental efficiency, although such a move is likely to be strenuously opposed by incumbents.

---

73 Gupta, R., 1995. 'Politics threatens Indian civil service', *Australian*, Sydney, 24 July.

Duty statements for each public service position should be mandatory, and promotions to levels should be discontinued forthwith—selection for senior positions should not be limited to one entry point and promotions should not be automatic. At each level of vertical movement efficiency should be the most important criteria for selection to encourage entry of new ideas from outside the service, and to encourage real achievers to move vertically irrespective of their service location and sector of employment.

The power to transfer officials is one of the weapons often used by politicians or senior officers to make bureaucrats and subordinate officers to follow their orders. To ensure that the threat of transfer cannot be used, the decision to transfer officers should be made by a departmental committee with staff representation to ensure adherence to predetermined guidelines on transfer policy. To be seen to be fair and to prevent any tendency for the committee to become a power house on staffing matters, its members should be required to rotate after a set period.

The current tendency of taking shelter behind the confidentiality clause to avoid justifying many bureaucratic actions should be replaced by a commitment to open government as far as practicable. The Freedom of Information act should make it difficult to deny the requested information without justifiable grounds.

Non-salary benefits to all public officials including senior bureaucrats should be determined annually by an independent agency. No payments should be allowed outside the parameters set by this agency. Payments made under this category should be made public at regular intervals. The current practice is riddled with corruption possibilities. One of the perks selectively available to politicians and bureaucrats is to seek medical treatment overseas. The press has reported a number of such expenditures by individual bureaucrats or politicians. For example, when per capita health expenditure by average Indians varied between Rs 15 to Rs 45 in 1986–87, the government approved generous funding assistance to current and former ministers, their wives, selected bureaucrats and many party officials to undertake medical treatment overseas. Some were granted funding assistance twice. The highest amount was granted to a junior minister who received Rs 4.5 million;

in some cases the concerned department was not even able to disclose the amount paid.[74]

Ministerial expenditure even in developed countries remains a thorny issue and thére are plenty of examples where ministers were sacked, forced to resign or even criminally prosecuted for small expenditures which were either not authorised or not allowable under existing guidelines. If this can be done in other countries, there is no reason why such a practice cannot be developed and implemented in India. The peoples' confidence can only increase when they find that every expenditure is authorised and documented and that guidelines are applied uniformly.

74 *The Statesman Weekly,* 1997. 'Government spends fortune on ministers' treatment', Calcutta, 13 September.

Appendix One

In the following major cases of corruption during the last decade all accused persons are either high powered politicians or captains of business, industry or senior bureaucrats.[75]

The Jain Hawla case involved payment of large funds to ministers and opposition politicians. Although some of the accused have been exonerated, the case still has not been concluded.

The St. Kits forgery case implicated a former prime minister. The accused former prime minister has been discharged but the case has not been brought to its final conclusion.

The Jharkhand Mukti Morcha bribery case in which a former prime minister was accused of buying votes of four members of parliament to defeat an opposition sponsored no confidence motion. This case has more twists and turns than many others. In court on 4 November 1997, the approver (a former Member of Parliament) also implicated the President of the Congress party who earlier was providing political support to the minority government, but in spite of this no charges have yet been laid against him.[76]

The Bihar animal husbandry scam involved about Rs 10,000 million. A large number of the accused are highly placed and among the principal accused are two former chief ministers. The main accused person has been released on bail and the common perception is that in spite of an unprecedented judicial role in this case to date, the case may not produce any result because of the softly, softly approach adopted by the prosecuting agency at the insistence of its political masters. There is much anecdotal evidence available such as

- the summary removal of the investigating agency's counsel who proved to be very effective in the initial stages of the case
- alleged harassment of the principal investigator of the case who has been universally credited for unearthing the scam (Irani 1997)

---

75 *India Today*, (1997). New Delhi, 14 July.
76 *The Statesman Weekly*,(1997). Calcutta, 8 November.

- the Governor's delaying tactics before giving approval to proceed with the prosecution of the highly placed persons and little cooperation from the senior state bureaucracy, who were alleged to have been hand picked by the accused when he was Chief Minister.[77]

The Bofors case relates to illegal commission of Rs 6,500 million paid to Indian intermediaries by the Swedish arms manufacturer to clinch a deal to supply armaments for the Indian army. The alleged recipients of the funds are alleged to be the front for a high profile senior political figure. The Swedish and the Swiss Government have cooperated with the Indian authorities to uncover this deal, and an official in the Swedish company has already dealt with by the Swedish legal system. Again this case has now been going for nearly a decade and in spite of various respectable investigative journalists' public assertions that enough evidence is available to prosecute the offending person or persons, the prosecuting agency is still to submit charge sheets against alleged offenders (Irani 1997).

Other major corruption cases yet to be resolved are a Rs 1,330 million urea import scam case and a Rs 13,336 million Indian Bank scam case, the Ashok Jain foreign exchange regulation violation case.

---

77 *The Statesman Weekly,* (1997). Calcutta, 1 November.

Appendix Two

Board of Revenue

The current board is an integral part of the executive. To an outsider the board has failed to perform its assigned tasks effectively. If it was functioning effectively, the question needs to be asked how nearly a quarter of the country's GDP remains undeclared even though everybody, including the officials, has been aware of the severity of the problem for more than three decades.

- Since 1965 the government has introduced four time-bound voluntary disclosure schemes asking holders of ill gotten/black money to declare their income, pay the due income tax on the declared amount and a guarantee that no questions will be asked as to the source of the declared income. The latest scheme expired in December 1997. The government claims that the latest scheme succeeded in unearthing a significant amount of black money. The question is how the government could declare the scheme successful when undeclared income of such a magnitude remained undetected for such a long-time. The latest amnesty netted an additional taxation revenue of Rs 100,500 million out of a total declared income of Rs 330,000 million.[78] The gravity of the tax evasion problem can be gauged from the fact that one individual alone paid a tax of Rs 1,750 million on a declared income of Rs 5,840 million,[79] when annual per capita GDP in India in 1993 was Rs 11,000.
- In 1964 the Santhaman Committee on corruption relating to government spending programs and the Wanchoo Committee report of 1969 on black-money aspects of direct taxation acknowledged the existence of a huge black economy. A government funded study in 1985 estimated ill-gotten and/or unreported income to be about one quarter of the GDP (Acharya 1985). This estimate is considered by economists and policy makers to be as accurate as one could be under the circumstances. If the findings of the study are accepted as a reasonable assessment of the situation, then amount of declared income to date is very small. GDP (at market prices) in 1995–

78 *The Economic Times,* (1998). New Delhi, 4 January.
79 *The Economic Times,* (1997). New Delhi, 25 December.

96 was estimated to be about Rs 11,495 billion, assuming an exchange rate of Rs 35 to one US dollar (World Bank 1997c). Accordingly, estimated undeclared income or ill gotten money therefore could be anything between Rs 2,300 billion to 2,874 billion. It is therefore within reason to conclude that either the current administration of the Board is extremely inefficient, or, alternatively, it is unable to perform its duties properly because of high level corruption within the organisation or an unholy nexus between the bureaucracy and politicians or both inefficient and corrupt.

- The claimed success of the scheme also highlights the self-serving nature of the Indian bureaucracy. While by any objective assessment, the tax collection agency responsible should be lambasted for its failure to check such large amounts of tax evasion for such a long time, on the contrary the officials concerned were rewarded with one month's tax-free salary in 1975, and negotiations are currently underway concerning the type and amount of reward to be given to the officials for their 1997 efforts.[80]
- Under this proposal if an autonomous body was given full responsibility and authority to perform this task, and remained answerable to Parliament it would be reasonable to expect that the situation would not have deteriorated to the extent it has today. Furthermore, responsibility for failure to perform the tasks required of the position(s) could have squarely put on the Board and the head of the agency.

Election Commission

Conducting an election in a vast country like India is a complicated task. With significant adult illiteracy and large-scale poverty, unscrupulous political leaders and candidates will make every effort to contaminate the election process for their own benefit. Perceptions of the integrity of an election are therefore very important if the values of a civil society and democracy are to triumph. The importance of community perceptions of elections is nicely summed up by the International Electoral Institute Commission. Its view is that the people participating in an election own it because they were the ones to say it was free and fair (International Electoral Institute Commission

80 *Ibid.*

1993). The Election Commission therefore must be respected and have the confidence of the community for its integrity, honesty and efficient performance. The Commission under the leadership of the previous Chief Commissioner (Seshan) earned the universal confidence of ordinary citizens. The current commission is also considered to be effective.

The commission as it is constituted now broadly follows the line suggested here except that members are appointed by the Government and hold office for six years or until a member reaches the age of 65.

One of the reasons often cited for election corruption is the huge election expenses required to be incurred by candidates or the party under which they seek election. To overcome this problem one or a combination of mechanisms suggested below could be implemented.

- State funding of election expenses based on a set formula, not allowing any private or public contribution to individual election funds. The main problem with this is that it would be too expensive, particularly in the context of competing demand for funds.
- Channeling election fund contributions through an arm of the Election Commission so that the source of every contribution is publicly known and political parties cannot hide contributions to election funds. This will reduce any inducement for elected members or political parities to return the favour to the contributor(s) after the election, thus reducing chances of corrupt practices.
- Allowing private funding of election expenses but stringently requiring all candidates to submit proof of all sources of election fund and accounting for all election expense. Failure to do so within a prescribed time or submitting an inaccurate return will lead to summary disqualification from membership and should be considered a criminal offence and severely dealt with under the full force of law. Furthermore, in the event a member is found to be disqualified, the person individually should be barred from seeking any public office for at least five years and the party concerned barred from contesting or endorsing any candidate for that or adjacent seats (in the event of an electoral redistribution of boundaries) for at least one term. Undoubtedly, the disqualification proposal is very punitive but when established

rules are violated by elected representatives, remedial measures equally need to be exemplary.

Anti-defection laws already exist; unfortunately they have not proved to be effective. Most of the political parties agree that drastic changes in the anti-defection law are needed and some even argue that the existing law is totally useless and should be scrapped.[81] The law needs to be made simple and stringent, although to a certain extent more stringent anti-defection rules on occasion may be contrary to the Westminster principle of members voting on issues without favour or fear. However, in modern parliamentary democracies where political parties dominate elections, only in exceptional cases are party whips not followed. Changing party allegiance during the tenure of a Parliament on ideological or policy grounds is understandable. However, in India's case it has been found that most shifts in allegiance were based on narrow self-interest or by offers of benefits including appointment to ministerial or similar public positions. This changing of allegiance not only creates instability, it encourages corruption and devalues the election process, and reduces the community's confidence in the democratic institution. Again, there cannot be a single full-proof mechanism. Modification of the present system could take one the following two forms.

Should a number of elected members collectively form a splinter group and wish to shift their allegiance to another group or join another group to form a government in defiance of the official position taken by the group under whose banner they were initially elected, the group members should resign their seats forthwith and seek fresh mandate from the electorate, should they intend to accept office or any other benefit during the life of the Parliament. If an individual member decides to resign from the party under whose umbrella the member was elected he/she should do the same. Should the defected member(s) decide not to resign, they can remain as member of the Parliament, but not be allowed to accept any benefit (e.g. in the form of ministerial appointment or chairperson of any committee or any other government or parliament appointed position) during the life of that parliament or assembly. However, should the concerned member(s) decide to resign and be re-elected under the banner of the new party or group then there should be no bar from accepting an office. This way, the temptation of

81 Kumar, P., 1997. 'Politicians insist bill should curb poll panel clout', *The Asian Age*, Calcutta, 31 July.

a ministerial berth or other benefits will not induce a member to defect for personal gains. The frequent change of government during the short-term of each of the three previous coalition governments could not have taken place if stringent regulations existed. Similarly, the appointment of 74 ministers in Bihar and 93 Ministers in the state of Uttar Pradesh in 1997 to ensure that there were no defections to the opposition or rewarding everybody who had already defected could have never taken place.

Comptroller and Auditor General (CAG)

The office is currently totally independent of the Executive. Performance of the previous holders of this position varied. There are instances when the office holder performed the duties of the position with distinction and there are occasions when the performance was sketchy. The focus of the position however remains to be recast to accommodate the rapidly changing financial environment in which modern governments are required to operate.

- The advent of computer technology makes financial auditing a relatively easy, mechanical task. However, even within this environment the vigilance and integrity of the system needs to be carefully observed and monitored. The new focus, in line with evolving international practices, is to be performance audit or evaluation of government programs, if the value for tax payers' funds are to assured. Given India's vast size and given that one single body is responsible for both federal and state auditing, it might be worthwhile to look at the possibility of establishing an auditing board similar to the Election commission.
- Currently the auditor's investigations are limited to ensuring that all paper work is accurate. The office does not make any physical check of whether the expenses were incurred as specified. This failure has led to, amongst other things, poor construction by using materials well below the specified quality and quantity. In this environment officials who resort to corrupt practices have been able to ensure that all paper work satisfies the auditors requirements, fully knowing that the corruption will remain undetected. However, if specific physical checks on project expenditures become normal practice this will provide an additional check against corrupt practices.
- An area which needs careful assessment by the Parliament is what happens after the Comptroller and Auditor General discover gross irregularities or inefficiencies either by the government or the bureaucracy. For example, in 1993 it found that the government suffered losses to the extent of Rs 34.42 billion (mainly because of faulty methods of sale of shares) and also provided evidence of under-realisation of disinvestment proceeds mainly due to faulty methods of valuations of shares (Ghuman 1997). By any definition this is a massive loss caused by inefficiency or corrupt practices. There are many such examples.

It is not publicly known whether any investigation took place to find out reasons for such gross mismanagement or whether any criminal charges were brought against the defaulting people. If the bureaucracy is allowed to remain unchallenged in the face of such massive mismanagement, no body in the world can initiate change. The act should empower the CAG to recommend binding punitive action if such inefficiencies are to be prevented from reoccurring in future.

Corporate Regulating Agency

Both national and multinational corporations exert significant influence at various levels of government and maintain close liaison with power brokers at the political and bureaucratic levels. At the same time since they operate in an international environment, they could (but do not necessarily) subvert government's legitimate taxation, environment and competition policies etc. The situation is further complicated by the differing focus of laws in the various countries within which they operate. In many countries self-regulatory mechanisms exist to control the misuse of corporate powers, and their effectiveness depends upon the environment in which they operate. This agency therefore must be responsible to Parliament to perform its tasks effectively without fear or favour.

Director of Public Prosecution (DPP)

This independent position is proposed to put an end to the current practice of politicians interfering with the investigating or prosecuting agency's work to protect highly positioned persons charged with criminal activities. Currently senior officials do not hold statutory office, and the responsible agency or the person often are faced with undue pressure to not proceed with an investigation or prosecute the alleged offender(s). To overcome this situation the DPP should be totally outside the executive's jurisdiction.

- The statutory responsibility of this position will be first, to decide whether investigation by the investigating agency was concluded on the basis of established best practices, if not what were their failures. It should also be able to direct further investigation to ensure that everything has been done properly.
- Second, on receipt of the investigating agency's report the office will independently decide whether prosecution should proceed and then conduct the prosecution case. It will be also be within the office's responsibility to decide whether an appeal should be lodged in a higher court against the judgement of a lower court. It will also follow the directions given by the executive to proceed on appeals against judgements of lower courts, should the executive feel that the penalty has been disproportionately lenient. In the event they decide to not proceed with prosecution on the basis of an investigator's report, the office will be required to give its reasoning in writing. Similarly, when there

exists public concern on the judgement of certain cases, the office will be required to give its decision in writing for the perusal of the community. In other words, the DPP's job is to bring back the public's confidence in the judicial process which has been severely dented by inept investigation, poor quality of prosecution and undesirable political interference in cases involved with powerful persons. Most importantly, it will stop politicians deciding whether a fellow politician is prosecuted. It was reported that the Central Bureau of Investigation (CBI) was ready to proceed with charges against a prominent state politician. However, because of alleged disagreement between law officers within the organisation it was left to the minister for law to decide. In this case severe doubts have been expressed in various quarters about the ultimate motive behind this move. Even if it is assumed that the minister has no ulterior motive, it puts the minister in an unenviable situation, and whatever decision he gives will not be seen as independent.

- The recent judgement of the three-judge bench of the Supreme Court on 18 December 1997 directing the government to appoint future director of the CBI illustrates how the present system has failed to earn people's confidence.[82] An independent DPP office will, to a large extent, remove some of the concerns expressed by the Division Bench's judgement.

Chief Statistician

The position should not only be independent, but must also be upgraded from its relatively junior position within the bureaucratic hierarchy. Statistics on various economic, social and administrative aspects are important guides to indicate the performance of a government. Data on the level of inflation and unemployment can be very sensitive in certain times (say close to an election), and governments are known to have made deliberate attempts either to suppress or manipulate data which could put them in an embarrassing situation. During a recent interview with some academics and middle-level government officials the author was shown examples of how some sensitive data were manipulated before they were available to public. If the position is made statutory, community confidence in

82 *The Hindu*, 1997. 'Greater freedom for CBI to probe graft cases', Chennai, 19 December.

sensitive statistical information will increase, and on occasions government will find it easier to explain difficult economic policies with comparative ease as people will be inclined to believe even unhelpful statistics if it is generated by an independent office. The controversy raised by the findings of the Gangopadhaya, Dubey and Jain study on the level of poverty and the failure of the Central Statistical Organisation to explain how it arrived at a higher figure although both the studies followed the same methodology gives credence to the argument that the CSO may not have always produced politically neutral data.

Ombudsman

This office is known as Lokpal in India. However, the focus of the office is different from what is normally understood elsewhere. For example, currently all complaints including complaints of corrupt behaviour against the members of Parliament are investigated by this office. All corruption investigations and charges need to be considered by one agency to ensure that a focus against corruption is maintained and cross-jurisdiction is avoided on criminal investigations. The ICAC (see below) would be a more appropriate agency to examine corrupt behaviour by public service officials, including Parliamentarians.

The function of the office should focus on the following and the office holder should directly report to the Parliament. Furthermore, there needs to be a legislative assurance that the Ombudsman's annual report along with its recommendations will be promptly addressed by the executive following consideration of the same by the Parliament.

The Ombudsman's functions should specifically focus on

- receiving and considering complaints against government's service delivery mechanism including failure to follow prescribed procedures and regulations
- investigation of all complaints by citizens against any unjust decision taken by government or any of its agents
- whether good governance practices (as commonly understood) are followed in serving the citizens by the government departments or agencies
- government departments and agencies, in the light of its own experience in dealing with complaints, to establish effective

internal complaint handling procedures and the delivery of service in line with their respective charters.

In discharging its functions properly and appropriately, the Office should ensure that firstly, good governance practices in preserving democratic values of the individual society or of its citizens are preserved at all costs; and secondly, it can work independently without showing any favour to anybody irrespective of agencies' or individuals' position and power in the government or in the society.

Human Rights Commission

India already has an Independent Human Rights Commission. It has earned a reputation for its independent stance in addressing Human Rights violation complaints. However, its reports virtually have remained ineffective as successive governments did not provide appropriate attention to its recommendations. Because of this the impact of the Commission has not been felt in society.

Similar to the office of the Ombudsman, its annual report should be considered by the Parliament and Parliament's decisions on the report should be binding upon the government. Failure to do so would lead to loss of faith on the Commission by citizens at large.

Independent Broadcasting Control Authority

The government had established an independent board known as the Prashar Bharati Board to manage all aspects of government owned broadcasting agencies (eg. All India Radio, Doordarshan). However, the executive head of the Board was appointed by the government.

However, unless the Board is given total autonomy including the power to appoint its own chief executive officer and other senior officers without any reference to the executive government, its independence will remain limited. To ensure its full independence, the Board should have this power as well as to decide its own priorities, independent of the executive, within the parameters set by its charter.

It is recently reported in the Press that the government wishes to appoint a Parliamentary committee to oversee the functions of the agency. If the functions of the mooted committee remains similar to that of a Parliamentary Select Committee, the proposal is unlikely to impact on the independence of the Board. If the intention behind this proposal is something else, then it might compromise the independence of the Board. The executive needs to consider this issue more carefully before proceeding with the idea to appoint a Parliamentary Committee to overview the Board's operations.

Independent Authority Against Crime and Corruption (ICAC)

A new and revamped criminal investigating agency to investigate corruption against publicly elected officials, senior bureaucrats and law enforcement agencies. Currently there exists a Central Vigilance Commission to investigate corruption. The Central Bureau of Investigation has been responsible for investigating cases of corruption in the public arena. The Bureau is required to seek government approval to investigate corruption cases against officers at the Joint Secretary level and above, and public office holders. Events during the last two decades in particular have established that both these agencies have not achieved any major success in their fight against corruption and criminal activities, particularly against people in high positions. Political leadership from the highest office of the land to ordinary members of the Parliament have all expounded the virtues of honest and clean government and spared no effort to invite ordinary citizens to fight against the evils of corruption. And yet, in a number of instances the leadership has acted differently either through their action or inaction when urgent decisions were required of them.

The CBI chief position has been subject to significant controversy in recent years, and in the opinion of many the position has been politicised by the executive to ensure that people in high places accused of high level corruption are protected from being brought before the law. During the last two decades a large number of corruption cases at the highest level have surfaced. Respected investigative journalists in India claim to be in possession of copies of documents with incriminating evidence of high level involvement in many of such corruption cases. Only a very few of the alleged perpetrators have been brought before the courts. There is anecdotal evidence that many of the investigations were not pursued with the vigour they deserved by the investigating agency. Decisions taken by governments from time to time in transferring senior officers at crucial juncture of investigation or sudden resignation of senior investigation officers with established reputation without any acceptable explanation confirm some of the suspicions that are rife.

The gravity of interfering in investigations against powerful community figures became clear when a division bench of the Supreme Court issued a clear direction of an unprecedented nature for executive's action. The Bench issued the direction while disposing a petition in a major corruption case seeking its orders to make the investigative agencies autonomous or at least independent. The Court's order indirectly acknowledged that the agency was indeed manipulated or influenced by people in high positions in the investigative work. The Court ordered that

- the government should give statutory status to the Central Vigilance Commission and its superintendence over the functioning of the Central Bureau of Investigation (CBI). From now onwards appointment to the Commission is to be made in consultation with a committee which should include the leader of the opposition. The CBI chief will be recommended by a committee headed by the Vigilance Commissioner, although the final selection should be made by the Appointment Committee of the Cabinet. If recommendations made by panels are found unacceptable, the reasons should be recorded and the Committee should be asked to draw up a fresh panel
- arbitrary transfer of the Directorate of the CBI and enforcement directorate should cease and occupants must be appointed for at least two years
- an independent panel of lawyers with impeccable integrity should be entrusted with the task of overviewing prosecution, similar to the Director of Prosecution in the United Kingdom.

The suggestions made earlier go beyond the order made by the Division Bench of the Supreme Court. The recent experience of the Asian economic crises, and the global concern over the Indonesian Government's response to the tough rescue measures insisted by the International Monetary Fund provide clear examples that if the government does not take effective measures to fight corruption, the international community at the first available opportunity will demand actions which will have the potential to create severe hardship to the community. India, in the eyes of the international financial agencies, business and government, non-government organisations is not far behind the critical point reached in Indonesia except that India has a relatively open government system in many respects. The measures suggested, if adopted and properly executed will assist in raising confidence in India by those who are not sure of the future at this point in time.

References

Acharya, S., (1985), *Aspects of Black Money in India*, National Institute of Public Finance and Policy, New Delhi.

Anita, N.H., (1997), 'Public health: hi-tech Western ideas irrelevant', *The Statesman Weekly*, 27 September, Calcutta.

Appleyard, R.T. and Stahl, C.W., (1995), *South Pacific Migration: New Zealand experience and implications for Australia*, AusAID, Commonwealth of Australia, Canberra.

Azad, M.A.K., (1960), *India Wins Freedom: an autobiographical narrative*, Longmans Green, New York.

Balfour, The Earl of (1936), 'Foreword', in Walter Bagehot, *English Constitution*, OUP, London.

Basu, K., (1997), 'Paying for education—leave higher learning to the market and primary education to the States', *India Today*, 17 November, New Delhi.

Bayley, D.H., (1983), *Police and Political Order in India*, Asian Survey, April. Quoted in Subramaniam (1992).

Bernard, J.A., (1996), 'Bengal and Punjab: before and beyond', *History Today*, Vol. 47 (9), September, History Today Ltd., London:28–33.

Bhagwati, J., (1995), *India in Transition—freeing the economy*, (paper back edition), Clarendon Press, New York.

——, (1996), *K.R. Narayan Oration*, The Australian National University, Canberra.

Bhargava, A., (1997), *Taxman*, Taxman Publications Ltd., New Delhi.

Bhatt, N., (1997), 'Microenterprise development and the entrepreneurial poor: including the excluded', *Public Administration and Development*, Vol. 17 No. 4, Wiley, London:371–86.

Bhattacharya, B.B., (1997), *Recent Institutional Reforms in India with particular reference to the Financial Sector*; at an international Seminar on South Asian Development in 1997 and Beyond: its Relevance for Australia at the University of Sydney, 12–14 September, Sydney.

Bhattacharya, P., (1997a), 'Whither Indian bureaucracy', *Statesman Weekly*, 13 September, Calcutta. A review article.

Boone, P., (1995), *Politics and the Effectiveness of Foreign Aid*, National Bureau of Economic Research, Cambridge, Mass.

Brown, J., (1997), 'Gandhi and Nehru: frustrated visionaries?', *History Today,* Vol. 47 (9), September, History Today Ltd., London:22–7.

Brummer, A. and Elliott, L., (1998), 'Ministers are proposing radical surgery', The *Guardian*. Reprinted in the *Canberra Times*, 31 January, Canberra.

Chakrabarti, S., (1997), 'Gold is old, but who'll tell Indians', *The Statesman Weekly*, 13 September, Calcutta.

Chatterjee, P.K., (1997), 'Corrupt legacy: need for healthy conventions', *The Statesman Weekly*, 8 November, Calcutta.

Chaube, S.K., (1997), 'President's rule: re-examining Article 356', *The Statesman*, 6 August, Calcutta.

Cleland, J., (1996), 'A regional review of fertility trends in developing countries: 1960–95', in Lutz., W. (ed.) *The Future Population of the World: what can we assume today,* Earthscan Publication Ltd., London:47–72.

Cohen, A., (1974), *Two Dimensional Man*, University of California Press, Berkeley.

Conor, A.E.W., (1989), 'Anti-corruption legislation: will more and better rules curb widespread corruption?', *East Asian Executive Reports*, January, Washington.

Cooke, J.E., (ed.), (1961), *The Federalist,* No. 78, Wesleyan University Press, Middletown, USA.

Criminal Justice Commission, (1990), Criminal JusticeCommission Queensland Annual Report 1989–90 (1990), Brisbane.

DAC (1993), Draft DAC Orientation Paper on Participatory Development and Good Governance, OECD, Paris (unpublished).

DAC (1995), *Participatory Development and Good Governance,* OECD, Paris:28–30.

Dasgupta, B., (1997), On South Asian Trade: the case for South Asian Free Trade Association at an international Seminar at the University of Sydney on South Asian Development in 1997 and Beyond: Its Relevance for Australia, 12–14 September, Sydney.

Davidson, B., (1992), *The Blackman's Burden*, Random House, New York.

Dubey, A. and Gangopadhaya, S., (1998), 'Poverty and economic reforms', in the *Economic Times*, 28 February, New Delhi.

Economic Times (1997), *RBI scales down GDP growth forecast to 6 per cent,* 26 November, New Delhi.

——, (1997a), 7 February.

——, (1997b), *FICCI Survey*, 24 December, New Delhi.

——, (1998), *Inflow of Foreign Capital into China at Record High*, 5 January, New Delhi.

Ekeh, P.P., (1975), Colonialism and the two publics in Africa: A theoretical statement, Comparative Studies in Society and History, 17; Quoted in May, R.J. in *Des Promesses A La Crise: Economic Politique De La Papousaie - Nouvelle - Guinee, Revue Tiers Monde*, Vol. XXXVIII No. 149:140–56 (English version).

Elek, A., [Ed], (1997), *A Matter of Evolution(Building on Asia-Pacific Community: Development Cooperation with APEC)*,The Foundation for Development Cooperation, Brisbane.

Elgardo, B., (1992), *Governance and Development: Issues and Constraints in the Proceedings of the World Bank Annual Conference on Development Economics 1991*, the IBRD/World Bank, Washington, DC.

Expert Group on the Commercialisation of Infrastructure Projects (1996), *The India Infrastructure Reports, Vols. I, II and III,* Ministry of Finance, Government of India, New Delhi.

Ghosh, A., (1997), *Indian Economy: its nature and problems*, New Book Stall, Calcutta.

Ghosh, R.N., (1977), *Agriculture in Economic Development*, Vikas Publishing House, New Delhi.

Ghuman, B.S., (1997), Public Enterprise Reform in India: Rhetoric and Reality in *The Review of Policy Issues,* Vol. 3 No. 1, Sheffield Hallam University, UK:29–40.

Government of India (1996), *The India Infrastructure Report, Vols. I, II and III*, Expert Group on the Commercialisation of Infrastructure Projects, Ministry of Finance, New Delhi.

——, (1997), *India 1996*, Publication Division, New Delhi.

Gupta, S. and Ghosh, S., (1992), *A Tract on Economic Development: Process and Perspective*, Charu Publishing Company, Calcutta.

Independent Commission Against Corruption, New South Wales *AnnualReport to 30 June 1989* (1989), Sydney.

Indira Gandhi Institute of Development Research (1997), *Indian Development Report 1997*, Mumbai (Bombay).

International Electoral Institute Commission (1993), *Free and Fair: Towards Democratic Governance*, Ministry of Foreign Affairs, Stockholm, Sweden.

Irani, C.R., (1997), 'Not centre-state relations, Prime Minister!', *The Statesman Weekly*, 11 October, Calcutta.

——, (1997a), 'Will Prime Minister Gujral please stand up?', *The Statesman Weekly*, 1 November, Calcutta.

——, (1997b), 'Under what law, Mr. Khalap?', *The Statesman Weekly*, 22 November, Calcutta.

——, (1998), 'For once, let the law take its course!', *The Statesman Weekly*, 31 January, Calcutta.

Kaul, M., (1997), The New Public Administration: management innovation in government; *Public Administration and Management*, Vol. 17 No. 1, London:13–26.

Kaul, S., (1997), *Villain of the Piece—on the Institution of Governor*, Hindustan Times, 27 November, New Delhi.

Kidwai, M.S., (1997), *Centre is Holding*, The Statesman Weekly, 13 December, Calcutta. A review article on Rethinking Indian Federalism Edited by Khan, Rasheeduddin.

Kilgaard, R., (1997), Cleaning up and invigorating the civil service in *Public Administration and Development*, Vol. 17 No. 5, Wiley, London:497–510.

Kohli, A., (1992), *Democracy and Discontent: India's Growing Crisis of Governability*, Cambridge University Press, Cambridge.

Leftwich, A., (1993), Governance, democracy and development in the Third World, *Third World Quarterly,* Vol. 14 No 3:605–24.

Lewis, J., P., (1995), *India's Political Economy—Governance and Reform*, OUP.

Lutz, W., Goldstein, J.R. and Prinz, C., (1996), Alternative Approaches to Population Projection in Lutz, W., (ed.), *Op. Cit*:14–44.

Maheswari, S.R., (1997), *Indian Administration—An Historical Account*, Jawhar Publishers, New Delhi.

Marshall, P., (1997), *The Making of the Hybrid Raj, 1700–1857*, History Today, Vol. 47 (9), September, London:4–9.

Migdal, J.S., (1988), *Strong Societies and Weak States: State Society Relations and State Capabilities in the Third World,* Princeton University Press, New Jersey.

Muganda, A.A., (1985), The Corruption Conundrum in Tanzania: Its Limits and Impact. Proceedings of the 7th UN Congress on the Prevention of Crime and Treatment of Offenders, Milan, Italy.

Mukarji, N., (1997), 'Pay Commission and all that', *Economic and Political Weekly*, 12 April, Mumbai (Bombay):750–3.

Mukherjee, S. and Mukherjee, I., (1995), *The Constitution of India*, World Press, Calcutta.

Mukhopadhaya, A.K., (1997), 'On the Kerala High Court Judgement 'in *Bartaman* (a metropolitan daily), 4 August, Calcutta.

Mustafa, S., (1997), 'The fault lies in the system, not in Laloo', *The Asian Age*, 2 August, Calcutta.

Naik, J.A., (1997), 'Workers earn more, farmers less', *The Statesman Weekly*, 6 September, Calcutta.

Narayan, H., (1997), 'Caste, creed and carnage', *The Statesman Weekly*, 13 December, Calcutta.

Nariman, F.S., (1998), 'Spirit of Freedom: the lost idealism', *The Statesman Weekly*, 13 September, Calcutta.

Nayar, B.R., (1975), *Violence and Crime in India: A Quantitative Study*, Macmillan, Delhi.

Noorani, A.G., (1973), *Ministers' conduct*, Vikash Publishing House, Delhi.

——, (1984a), *President's Rule in the States*, Indian Express, 6 February. Also, reprinted in The Indian Affairs: The Constitutional Dimension, Konark Publishers, Delhi.

——, (1984b), *Is the Constitution Eroding?*, Indian Express, 24 April. *Ibid.*

——, (1987), *Constitution and Civil Servants*, Indian Express 27 February, New Delhi. Also, reprinted in The Constitutional Dimension, *Ibid.*

——, (1988), President's Right to Know, the Indian Express, 18 March, New Delhi. Also, reprinted in Indian Affairs: The Constitutional Dimension, *Ibid.*

——, (1989a), *The President and the Constitution*, Indian Express, 12 May. Also, reprinted in The Indian Affairs; *Op. cit.*.

——, (1989b), *Forty Years of the Constitution*, 26 November, Sunday Mail, London. Also, reprinted in the Indian Affairs; *Ibid.*

——, (1989c), *The Presidential System: The Indian Debate*, Sage Publishers, London.

Ostergaard, C., S., (1986), Explaining China's recent political corruption, *Corruption and Reform*, Martinus Nijhoff Publishers, Dordrecht.

Pai Panandiker, D.H., (1997), Trends in Trade, *The Hindustan Times*, 15 December, New Delhi.

Pai Panandiker, V.A., (1989), In his Foreword to *The Presidential System: The Indian Debate*, Noorani, A.G., *Op. cit.*

Panth, N., (1979), *Some aspects of irrigation administration* (a case study of Kosi project), Anugraha Narayan Sinha Institute of Social Studies, Patna.

Parthasarathy, G., (1996), *Federalism: Comparative Perspective from India and Australia* in a seminar on the same subject, Monash University, Melbourne.

Peak, R., (1997), IMF warns on global fall-out from Asia, *Canberra Times*, 22 December, Canberra.

Potter, D., (1986), *India's Political Administration 1991–1983*, Clarendon Press, Oxford.

Rangnekar, S., (1998), Loss-stricken Whirlpool to defer royalty payment, *The Economic Times*, 24 December, New Delhi.

Ray, B., (1995), *Diversity in Recruitment and Retention Practices and Representivity,* Paper presented at an international seminar organised by the South African Government and the Commonwealth Association for Public Administration and Management, 7–10 June, Capetown.

Ray, B. and May, R., (1996), 'Reforms in the public service: are we on the right track?', *Development Bulletin*, Volume 38, July 1996:47–50.

——, (1998), *Indian Ocean Rim Countries: Policy Challenges for Sustainable Development*, Indian Ocean Centre, Curtin University, Perth.

Ray, B. and Ghosh, R.N., (1997), 'Sustainable development in India: economic and administrative reforms—a precondition', in Roy, K.C., Blomqvist, H.C. and Hossain, I., (eds), *Development That Lasts*, New Age International, New Delhi.

Root, H.L., (1996), *Small Countries, Big Lessons, Governance and Rise of East Asia*, OUP, Hong Kong.

Rosengrant, M.W., (1997), *Water Resources in the 21st Century: Challenges and implications for action*, International Food Policy Research Institute, Washington, DC.

Roy, A.K., (1997), *What is the way to end corruption*?, Hindustan Times, 13 December, New Delhi.

Rustamji, K.F., (1997), *A 21st Century doctrine*, Hindustan Times, 10 October, New Delhi.

Ruzindana, A., (1995), 'Combating corruption in Uganda', in Langseth, P., Katorobo, J., Brette, E. and Muenne, J., (Eds), *Uganda: Landmarks in Rehabilitating a Nation*; Fountain Publishers, Kampala:191–208.

Sarkaria, Mr. Justice R.S., (1988), *Report of the Commission on Centre-State Relations*, Ministry of Finance, Government of India, New Delhi.

Sahay, K.B., (1997), *Family Planning: A Miserable Failure in India*, The Statesman Weekly, 6 September, Calcutta.

Seidman, A. and Seidman, R.B., (1994), *State and Law in the Development Process*, St. Martins Press, New York.

Sen, A.K., (1984), *Poverty and Famines: an essay in entitlement and deprivation*, Clarendon Press, Oxford.

Sen, S., (1997), *Paltry provision from 'evil practice'*, The Statesman Weekly, 5 April, Calcutta.

Singer, H.W., (1993), 'International governance—intentions and realities', *Development and International Cooperation, Vol. IX No. 16* (September):25–34.

Singh, P. and Bhandarkar, A., (1997), *IAS Profile: Myths and Realities,* Wiley Eastern, New Delhi.

Solow, R.M., (1996), *Intergenerational Equity, Yes—but what about inequity today?* UNDP (1996).

Subramaniam, K.S., (1992), *Political Violence, Social Movements and the State in India*, Institute of Development Studies, University of Sussex, Brighton.

Thistlewaite, B. and Davis, D., (1996), *Pacific 2010—A sustainable future for Melanesia*, National Centre for Development Studies, The Australian National University, Canberra.

Transparency International, (1997). *Annual Report*, Berlin.

United Nations (1990), *Corruption in Government: Report of an Interregional Seminar*, The Hague, Netherlands, 11–15 December 1989, New York.

——, (1995), *Background paper prepared by the Secretariat on international action against corruption* for the Ninth UN Congress on the Prevention of Crime and the Treatment of Offenders, Cairo (A/CONF 169/14).

——, (1995b). *World Population Prospects, 1994 Revision*, New York:144).

——, (1996), General Assembly Resolution 50/225, *Public Administration and Development, Vol. 16 No. 5,* London:513–6.

UNDP (1990), Human Development Report, OUP, New York.

——, (1996), *Human Development Report*, OUP, New York.

——, (1997), *Human Development Report*, OUP, New York.

Varshney, A., (1984), 'Political economy of slow industrial growth in India', *Economic and Political Economy*, 1 September, Mumbai (Bombay):1511–7.

Wade, Robert, (1984), *The Market for Public Office: why the Indian state is not better at development*, Institute of Development Studies, The University of Sussex, England.

Walker, J.P., (1996), *New Growth Theory and Development Assistance*, Department of Foreign Affairs and International Trade, Ottawa, Canada.

Wettenhall, R., (1996), Surveying Administrative Reform Across Commonwealth Countries, *Public Administration and Development, Vol. 16 No. 5*, London:517–9.

Wilson, Sir Harold, (1982), The Times, 6 February, London. Quote in Noorani (1994), *Op. cit.*

World Bank (1989), *Sub-Saharan Africa: From Crisis to Sustainable Growth*, Washington, DC.

—— (1992), *Governance and Development*, Washington, DC.

—— (1994a), *Development Practice, Governance. The World Bank's Experience*, Washington, DC.

—— (1994b), *World Development Report 1994. Infrastructure and Development*, OUP, New York.

—— (1995), *World Tables,* John Hopkins University Press, Baltimore.

—— (1997a), *World Development Report: The State in a changing World*, OUP, New York.

—— (1997b), *India - Achievements and Challenges in Reducing Poverty*, Washington, DC.

—— (1997c), *India 1997 Economic Update: Sustaining Rapid Growth*, Washington, DC.

—— (1997d), *World Development Indicators,* Washington, DC.

World Commission on Environment and Development (1987), *Our Common Features* (Australian edition). The Report is also known as *Brundtland Report*, named after the Chairman of the Commission Gro Harlem Brundtland, OUP, Melbourne.

World Resources Institute (1994), *World Resources 1994 - 95*, OUP, New York.

Wright, L., (1998), *IMF: new imperialistic force threatening to change the face of Asia*, The Canberra Times, 17 January, Canberra.

Xin, Ren, (1997), *Tradition of the Law and Law of the Tradition*, Greenwood Press, London.

Index